Lessons from the Apostle Paul's Prayers

Charles Haddon Spurgeon

Lessons from the Apostle Paul's Prayers

ISBN: 9781980344537

All Scripture is taken from the *King James Version.*

Material sourced from The Metropolitan Tabernacle Pulpit Sermons

CONTENTS

SERIES INTRODUCTION

The Rich Theology Made Accessible Series seeks to bolster the faith of busy Christians by making rich theology from time past more accessible.

Current Titles:

- Volume 1: *The Chief Exercise of Faith: John Calvin on Prayer*
- Volume 2: *Gospel Hope for Anxious Hearts: Trading Fear and Worry for the Peace of God* by Charles Spurgeon
- Volume 3: *Encouraged to Pray: Classic Sermons on Prayer* by Charles Spurgeon
- Volume 4: *Lessons from the Apostle Paul's Prayers* by Charles Spurgeon
- Volume 5: *Our Savior's Cries from the Cross* by Charles Spurgeon
- Coming Soon: Two works by Charles Spurgeon on the Holy Spirit

Visit Cross-Points.org/richtheology to learn more or to explore additional titles.

FOREWORD

Why study and pray the prayers of the Apostle Paul? One word: transformation. Of the many benefits we have in learning from Paul, a few stand out:

1. We see how the Holy Spirit wants us to pray.

Scripture provides a wealth of prayers inspired by the Holy Spirit, each of them giving a glimpse into the unsearchable wisdom of Almighty God. These prayers should shape our priorities and our entire outlook on life.

So often, we pray such small, self-centered prayers instead of asking how God would have us pray. As we read and pray Paul's prayers, God will work His purposes in us as we contemplate what Paul prayed for and why. Paul prayed for the eyes of Ephesian hearts enlightened (Ephesians 1:18) and rejoiced in the rich fellowship he had with the Thessalonian church (1 Thessalonians 3:9–13). When was the last time you prayed for either of those things?

Spurgeon illustrates why we want to pray according to God's priorities: "A man might try to fill us and fail, but God, who made us, knows every corner and cranny of our nature, and can pour in joy and peace till every portion of our being is flooded, saturated, and overflowed with delight."

2. We can pray along with Paul confident of God's answers.

Praying God's prayers according to God's priorities means we can be sure of God's answers. This doesn't mean He will answer as we expect, but it does mean God will answer prayers according to His will as He promises (1 John 5:14). Since Scripture is His revealed will, praying Paul's prayers guarantee God's answers.

Let this sink into your soul. As you earnestly pray for God to strengthen your faith to grasp the depths and riches of Christ's love (Ephesians 3:14–19), God will answer you— He wants you to experience the profundity of Christ's love.

"Expect great things, expect things beyond all expectation," Spurgeon writes. "Your largest hopes shall all be exceeded. Hope, and hope, and yet hope again, and each time hope more and more, but the Lord will give you more than you have hoped for."

3. Our minds will be enlightened and affections stirred.

As we contemplate the prayers and petitions of the great apostle, God's Spirit will illuminate the prayers and shape the desires of our heart. Instead of merely praying for circumstances and our to-dos, our hearts will pray for things like the filling of our minds with "the knowledge of His will in all spiritual wisdom and understanding, so as to walk in a manner worthy of the Lord, fully pleasing to him..." (Colossians 1:9). Praying these prayers will draw us into deeper delight and communion with our Father.

Lessons from The Apostle Paul's Prayers isn't a comprehensive study on the subject, but rather eight sermons working through rich nuggets from Paul's prayers.

Don't read this book to finish; read to change. Note helpful verses and quotes and incorporate them into your daily prayer routine. Put down the book and get on your knees. Cry out to God in worship, dependence, and intercession. He will hear you and He will answer.

The prayer of Paul in Philippians 1:9–11 is our prayer for this volume:

"And it is my prayer that your love may abound more and more, with knowledge and all discernment, so that you may approve what is excellent, and so be pure and blameless for the day of Christ, filled with the fruit of righteousness that comes through Jesus Christ, to the glory and praise of God."

—

The Editors at Cross-Points Books
Schaumburg, IL
January 2018

1
THE THREE WHATS

"The eyes of your understanding being enlightened; that ye may know what is the hope of his calling, and what the riches of the glory of his inheritance in the saints, and what is the exceeding greatness of his power to us-ward who believe, according to the working of his mighty power, which he wrought in Christ, when he raised him from the dead, and set him at his own right hand in the heavenly places."—Ephesians 1:18–20.

"The Lord must first enlighten the eyes of our understanding, or else, however precious the truth, and however clearly it may be stated, we shall never be able to apprehend it."

—

YOU see the text begins with a personal experience within the mind and judgment—"the eyes of your understanding being enlightened." Everything depends upon the opened eye: the scene may be fair, and the light may be bright, but if the sight be gone all is in vain. Zedekiah had his eyes put out by the king of Babylon, and then he was taken down to the imperial city, but for aught he could enjoy of all its splendour he might as well have been in a desert. There were vast halls and palaces, and hanging gardens and a city wall which was the wonder of the world, so that Babylon is called by the prophet "the glory of kingdoms and the beauty of the Chaldees' excellency"; but the blinded monarch beheld nothing of all the grandeur of the golden city, and to him her wealth was as though it had not been. Thus is it with us by nature, we have no apprehension of spiritual things, no power to discern eternal good, but our foolish heart is darkened. Therefore the Lord must first enlighten the eyes of our understanding, or else, however precious the truth, and however clearly it may be stated, we shall never be able to apprehend it.

I find there is a rendering of the text which runs thus, "The eyes of your heart being enlightened," and it strikes me that this version has about it the appearance of being the correct one, because divine things are usually better seen by the heart than by the understanding. There are a thousand things which God has revealed which we shall never understand, and yet we can know them by a loving, trustful experience. Our Saviour says, "Blessed are the pure in heart, for they shall see God." The purifying of the heart is the enlightening of the spiritual eye. Strange as it may seem, the true eye of the renewed man is seated rather in the heart than in the head: holy affections enable us to see, and as far as possible to understand divine things. I pray that in each one of us the eyes of our heart may be enlightened, that we may know spiritual things as they are best known.

Now, the prayer of our text was offered for Christians—
for converted persons, for those who had faith in Christ
Jesus and love to all the saints; yet Paul says that he never
ceased to pray that their eyes might be enlightened. Yes,
brethren, he who sees most needs to have his eyes
enlightened to see more, for how little as yet of the glory
of God have any of us beheld! Even that favoured pilgrim
who has been led by the shepherds to the top of Mount
Clear, to stand there with telescopic glass and gaze into the
glories of Immanuel's land, has yet only commenced to
perceive the things which God has prepared for them that
love him. I pray God that if we do already see, we may see
more, until our eye shall be so strengthened that the light
of the New Jerusalem shall not be too strong for us, but
amid the splendour of God which outshines the sun we
shall find ourselves at home.

But if believers need to have their eyes enlightened, how
much more must those who are unconverted. They are
altogether blinded, and consequently their need of
enlightenment is far greater. They were born blind, and the
god of this world takes care yet further to darken their
minds. Around them there broods a sevenfold midnight,
the gloom of spiritual death. "They meet with darkness in
the daytime, and grope in the noonday as in the night." O
blind eye, may Jesus touch thee! May the Spirit bring his
sacred eye-salve and make thee see, and to-night though it
is not ours to give thee eyes, we would tell thee what is to
be seen, hoping that, peradventure, while we give the
description, God may give thee eyes with which to verify
our report. Perhaps even the reporting of these things may
set thee longing for them, and, when thou hast but a

3

longing, God will hear thee. If that longing be turned into a prayer, and that prayer be kindled by a spark of faith, that longing shall be the beginning of light to thy soul, and thou shalt see the salvation of God.

To-night, then, there are two things we shall ask about, what things are to be seen and known according to the text; and, secondly, why it is our anxious desire that every person here should see and know these things.

I. First, then, WHAT IS TO BE SEEN AND KNOWN ACCORDING TO THE TEXT? When you heard me read it, you must have noticed that it contains three "whats." "The eyes of your understanding being enlightened that ye may know what is the hope of his calling, and what the riches of the glory of his inheritance in the saints, and what the exceeding greatness of his power to us-ward who believe." Upon these three "whats" I shall try to speak to-night, and may the Holy Ghost speak through me to all your souls.

Our first point is, "What is the hope of his calling?" A great many persons never think about religion, because they cannot believe that there is much in it. If they had half an idea of what is to be gained by it even now, and of the unspeakable blessedness which will come of it throughout eternity, surely their own desire to benefit themselves would incline them diligently to consider it, even if they went no further. So promising a matter is at least worth looking into, for it would be a great pity to miss present and eternal happiness if it can be had. But no, they suppose it to be a very small and trifling thing, fit only for the thoughts of priests and women, and such weak folk, and so they neglect it, despise it, and look after other business. To-night, while I try to tell what is the hope of the Christian man's calling, I boldly claim your best consideration. If the preacher may not request it on his own account he may assuredly ask it on the ground that his theme deserves it. Perhaps while we are speaking of the worth of this hope, and you are lending an attentive ear, the Lord may lead you to seek his face. Is it not written "Incline your ear and come unto me, hear and your soul shall live"? Many a man has been tempted to start upon a voyage by hearing much of the land to which he sails. Praise his goods and you will find the merchant buyers. Such is our desire at this time: we would so speak of the hope of our calling as to allure those who are eager after sweets to taste and see that the Lord is good.

The idea of the text seems to me to be illustrated well by the patriarch Abraham. Abraham was living in his father's house in Ur of the Chaldees when a call came to him. That call came from God. He was to separate himself entirely and to get away to a land which he had never seen. What was the hope of that calling? It was the hope that God would give him a seed, and give to that seed a land to dwell in. Thus spake the Lord unto him: "I will make of thee a great nation, and I will bless thee, and make thy name great; and thou shalt be a blessing: and I will bless them that bless thee, and curse him that curseth thee: and in thee shall all families of the earth be blessed." The great nation which should spring from him would possess the land in which he was to wander as a pilgrim and a stranger, according to the word of the Lord—"For all the land

5

which thou seest, to thee will I give it, and to thy seed for ever." For the sake of that hope he forsook everything, and dwelt in tents, a pilgrim and a sojourner with God, living entirely by faith, but living grandly and sublimely, and thus becoming the father of all believers throughout all ages, greater than a prince among the sons of men. Now, there comes to every man who is a true Christian a call from God. We speak of it by the name of "effectual calling." The Spirit of God personally applies the truth of Scripture to the heart, and makes the chosen man to feel that it belongs to him. The believer perceives that he is separated from others by the sovereign grace of God, and that therefore he must come out from the world, and no longer live according to the sight of the eyes and the hearing of the ears, but must live by faith upon God, as seeing him who is invisible. This makes the believer very different from the rest of mankind. Those who walk by sight do not understand him. They generally misrepresent him, and frequently they hate him, but he is content to be unknown, for he remembers it is written, "Ye are dead, and your life is hid with Christ in God." "Therefore the world knoweth us not because it knew him not."

But what is the prospect which leads the believer to this life? What is the hope of his calling? Brethren, let me describe the hope of those of us who have come out to walk by faith in Christ Jesus. We have already obtained enough abundantly to reward us for obedience to the call, and even if nothing were shut up in the closed hand of Hope, her open hand has greatly enriched us. Christian man, you have in possession already the forgiveness of your sin, acceptance in Christ, adoption into the divine family, and the nature, rank, and rights of a child of God. You already possess that which makes you amongst the happiest of mankind, and often do you feel that if it should turn out that there is no hereafter and if you should die like a dog, yet still your faith in God has given you such consolation and such strength, such peace and such joy that you would bless God that ever you had it. Our hope has not injured us either as to character or to happiness, and even if it turned out to be false we are at least as well off as the unbeliever. Still our main possession lies in hope. We carry a bag of spending money in our hands, but the bulk of our wealth is deposited in the Bank of Hope. What then is the Christian's hope?

Well, first, he hopes and believes that he shall be under divine protection for ever and ever, that he shall be the object of divine love time out of mind, and when time shall be no more. He hopes that all things shall work together for his good in the future as he perceives they have done in the past, and as he is persuaded they are doing now. He expects a stormy voyage, but because Christ is at the helm he hopes to come to the fair havens at the last. He expects to be tempted, but he hopes to be upheld. He expects to be slandered, but he hopes to be cleared. He expects to be tried, but he hopes to triumph. Sustained by this hope he dreads no labours and fears no difficulties.

> "He holds no parley with unmanly fears,
> Where duty bids be confidently steers,
> Faces a thousand dangers at her call,
> And, hoping in his God, surmounts them all."

His hope is that all through life, whether that be long or short (and he has not much care about the number of his years), underneath him will be the everlasting arms. He hopes that the Lord will be his shepherd, and he shall not want. He hopes that goodness and mercy will follow him all the days of his life. Hence he is not afraid to die, for then he expects to come into actual possession of his best possessions. He looks for his best things last. He believes that when it is time for him to depart, Jesus will come and meet him, and the thought of that meeting puts aside all idea of the grim terrors of the grave. His hope leaps over the grave, and lands him in a glorious resurrection. Does not the hope of our calling open grandly?

We hope also, and have good ground for it, that after death at the day of judgment we shall have, as we believe we have now, a perfect justification. A dread assize will be held. Upon a great white throne reflecting all things, and brilliant with its purity, Jesus the Judge of all will sit, and he shall separate the mass of mankind into two portions as a shepherd divides the sheep from the goats. We know that in that day he will discern those who believed in him and trusted him and obeyed him and sought to be like him, and we hope that we shall be of that blessed number. For us there shall be no sentence of condemnation, for it is written, "There is therefore now no condemnation to them which are in Christ Jesus." We hope for a sentence of acquittal, and we therefore challenge the judgment which others dread. Clothed with a righteousness divine we await with expectation the day which shall make the impenitent wish that they had never been born. Hope takes into her consideration the most dreaded of all events, and weaves it into her song. The end of all things is not the end of hope. Is not this brave hoping? The hope of a man who sings on for ever,—living in the circle of divine love, dying beneath the protection of divine power, and abiding in the judgment justified by divine justice: accepted in the beloved, and beloved of the Father.

What else hope we for? We hope for absolute perfection. The God who has changed our hearts will continue the good work of sanctification till he has taken every sin out of us, every desire for sin, every possibility of sin. We expect him to renew our minds and prevent our making so many mistakes in judgment. We expect him to renew our hearts that they may be wholly set on divine and heavenly things. We expect him to renew our entire spirit till when the prince of this world comes he shall find nothing in us—no tinder for his sparks, no corruption in which to sow his evil seed. We hope to be perfect, even as God is perfect. As Adam, when he came from his Maker's hand, so shall we be, and something more, for we shall possess a life in Christ which our unfallen progenitor knew not in Paradise.

We hope, also, that this body of ours will be perfected. It will lie in the grave and moulder into dust, unless our Lord Jesus should come before our death hour. Of this we make small account, having no very intense desire to avoid the grave wherein our glorious Redeemer lay. We have nothing to lose, but much to gain, by dying, for therein we put off our mortality that at the resurrection we may put on immortality.

"Corruption, earth, and worms
Shall but refine this flesh,
Till when the Lord our Saviour comes
We put it on afresh."

We expect that this our body shall be raised—changed, but still the same as to identity. For us is the promise of the Scripture—"I will ransom them from the power of the grave; I will redeem them from death." When our body awakes, though sown in corruption it shall be raised in incorruption, though sown in weakness it shall be raised in power, though sown a body only fit for the soul it shall be raised a body meet for our highest nature, even for our spirit. As we have borne the image of the earthy we shall also bear the image of the heavenly. Our body shall be fashioned like unto the body of Jesus Christ himself. We are looking forward to a time when we shall have done with aches and pains, with weariness and decay, with old age and its infirmities, and with all liability to death. We expect perpetual youth to be our portion, and that joy shall thrill through every nerve and sinew of our frame, which now, alas, so often becomes the theatre of agony. Yes, this is our hope, perfection of spirit, soul, and body; for Christ has redeemed the whole, and he will have the whole to be his inheritance, and in the whole of our manhood his glorious image shall be reflected for ever.

What else is the hope of our calling? Why, that being thus cleared in judgment and made absolutely perfect, we shall for ever—for eternal duration is the glory of our heritage—we shall for ever enjoy infinite happiness. We do not know what form the joys of eternity will take, but they will take such form as shall make us the most happy. We shall have heaven's best, yea God's best, and what that is who among us can guess, though he use all his knowledge and give the reins to his expectancy? "Eye hath not seen, nor ear heard, neither hath entered into the heart of man the things which God hath prepared for them that love him; but he hath revealed them unto us by his Spirit," and, as far as we understand that revelation we are taught by it that we shall enter into a state of complete rest and perfect peace; a state of holy delight, and of serene and blissful activity; a state of perfect praise; a state of satisfaction; a state, probably, of progress, but still of completeness at every inch of the road; a state in which we shall be as happy as we are capable of being, every vessel, little or great, being filled to the brim. We shall be supremely blessed, for at the right hand of God there are pleasures for evermore. This is the hope of our calling.

Nor even now have we come to an end, for something more yet remains. You say, "Can more be?" Yes, we expect for ever to be in a condition of power, and honour, and relationship to God. We hope to be brought so near to God that all the universe shall distinctly see that we are courtiers of the palace of the great King, yea, princes of the blood royal of the skies. We shall be very near to God, for we shall be with Jesus where he is, and sit upon his throne. We shall serve our God, and see his face while we serve him; and his glory will be reflected upon us and from us, and we shall be his dear sons and daughters in Christ Jesus for ever and ever. There is not an angel in heaven with whom the meanest saint might wish to change estates, for though the angels excel us now, we shall certainly excel them in the world to come: we shall be nearer the eternal throne than any one of them, inasmuch as Christ Jesus is our brother and not the brother of angels. He is God-and-man in one person, and there was never God and angel in like union, We shall be next to the Creator—let us speak it with bated breath but leaping heart—we shall be next to the eternal God, one with his only-begotten Son, who is one with himself. This is the hope of our calling.

Oh, sirs, is not this worth the having? Is not this worth striving for? When you count the cost, what cost is worth the counting? Might not a man for this lay down all that he has, yea, and his life also, to keep this pearl of exceeding price? And what if you should miss it? What, if you should miss it? What, if it could be proven, as it never will be, that there are no pains of hell and no eternal wrath, yet is not this enough—to have lost this immortality of glory, this immortality of honour, and of likeness to God? This pain of loss, may none of us ever incur it: for it is hell to lose heaven, it is infinite misery to miss infinite felicity. To be within an inch of an immortality of bliss and honour, and yet to let it slip by, will not this be an endless torment to the soul? To clutch the pleasures of an hour, all earth-stained as they are, shall we renounce the ecstacies of eternity? To snatch at bubbles which break ere we can grasp them, shall we let unfading glories go? For the mere sake of dwelling at ease by escaping thought shall we let boundless blessings run by us, counting ourselves unworthy of them, and so losing them? I do pray that you may know "what is the hope of his calling," and that when you know it you may cry, "I will have it. If it is to be had, by God's grace, I will have it now." So may it be, for Christ's sake.

And now I turn to the second "what" of the text, and that is more marvellous still. I am sure I cannot preach the text out, it is too great for me; but here it is—"That ye may know what are the riches of the glory of his inheritance in the saints."

Mark well that God's people are by grace made to be his saints, his select, his holy ones, and then they are viewed as his inheritance. The whole world is God's. The cattle on a thousand hills and all lands and seas are his, and yonder starry worlds which in profusion are sown in space are all his, but he deigns to call sanctified men and women his inheritance in a special sense. They are his peculiar treasure, his crown-jewels, dear and precious to him. "The Lord's portion is his people, Jacob is the lot of his inheritance." I want you to think of this grand truth, because practical results flow from it. If you and I are believers in Jesus we are God's inheritance, and the Lord has what the apostle calls "the riches of the glory of his inheritance in the saints." But how can God make riches out of poor men and women? They are believers in Jesus, but what is there in them that he counts to be riches—riches of glory, too?

We answer, first, he has spent riches of love upon them, for he loves them, poor as they are, and sick and sorry as they often are. He loved them from before the foundation of the world: and you know how precious a thing becomes when you love it. It is a beloved keepsake, and you would not part with it for a mint of gold. It may have little intrinsic value, but if you have long set your heart upon it how dear it becomes to you. God has loved his people so long and so intensely, with such an unbounded love, that there is a wealth in them to his heart. Oh, that we knew something of "the riches of the glory of his inheritance in the saints" as measured by the gauge of love.

Moreover, the Lord has spent a wealth of wisdom on his saints. A material may be almost valueless at first, but when a wise man has exercised his thought and skill upon it, the value may be enhanced a thousand-fold. But God has thought of his saints for ever. Eternal wisdom found her delights with the sons of men and occupied herself on their behalf before the foundation of the world. "How precious also are thy thoughts unto me, O God, how great is the sum of them!" God's wisdom has exhibited itself at its full in the plan of redemption. I scarcely hear of his deliberating for any purpose except for the salvation of his people, but in that matter we continually read of "the counsel of his will," to show us that, speaking after the manner of man, the Lord has reasoned within himself how best to save his own people. His thoughts of wisdom and prudence have been exercised upon his saints, and hence it is that there is a riches of glory about them.

What is more, when the riches of his love, and of his wisdom, had been expended it came to pass that it was necessary that he should spend a life of suffering upon them. Look ye to the glorious landscapes of rock and hill, and dale and mountain; turn your eye from grassy slope to snowy summit sparkling in the sun, and while ye admire all things remember that God hath costlier works than these. None of these cost the Lord an incarnation and a death. Look, if ye will, to all the majestic halls of heaven, where the lamps of glory are lit with supernal splendour, but neither angel, nor cherubim, nor seraphim cost their Lord a bloody sweat. Then look you at his people; view "his inheritance in the saints," for it is there that the Son of God, taking upon himself human nature, sighed and groaned and sweat great drops of blood, and felt the agonies of death. As the Lord looks over all that he has made he sees nothing that has cost him suffering and death till he comes to his people. Jesus knows what the saints cost him. He estimates them at a rate usual among men, for men say, "The price is what it will fetch," and Jesus knows what his people fetched when he redeemed them by giving himself for them. Measured by that standard God hath indeed riches of glory in his inheritance in the saints.

And then there comes great glory to God from the workmanship which he puts into his people. When he made the world it was with a voice. "He spake, and it was done." When he made the things that are he had but to will and they stood forth, but in the making of a Christian it needs the labour of the Godhead: Father, Son and Holy Spirit must all work to create a new creature in Christ Jesus. The Father must beget, the Son must redeem, the Spirit must regenerate; and when this is done the Godhead's omnipotence must be put forth to keep a Christian alive, and to perfect him, and present him "faultless before the presence of God with exceeding joy." An artisan can put into a small piece of iron, of no worth at all, so much labour that it shall be valued at scores of pounds, and the Triune God can expend so much workmanship upon our poor nature that a man shall be more precious than the gold of Ophir. Valued thus, the Lord may well speak of "the riches of the glory of his inheritance in the saints."

Now, as I want if I can to lead you into a sense of this glory for a minute, I should like you to accompany me while I speak somewhat carefully but yet enthusiastically about what the Christian becomes when God has perfected his work upon him.

Notice, then, that when at the last the believer shall have been perfected by the work of the Spirit, as he will be, man will be an extraordinary creature. Look ye. God has made matter, and upon matter has impressed his will, and from the tiniest drop to the mightiest orb, matter never disobeys the law which God imposes upon it. This is a great triumph. Call it "the law of gravitation," or what you will, it is quite certain that all inanimate nature is put under law by the Most High and that it never rebels. Huge as this great universe is, God has as complete power over it, as you have over the ball which you toss in your hand. This is glorious, but still it is small glory compared with that which God obtains from his people when they arrive at heaven, for they will not be mere dead, inert matter governed by laws, but they will be full of life and moral freedom, and yet they will be as completely subject to the divine mind as are the atoms of matter. This will be an achievement indeed—to have produced free agents which will be under no control of force, but perfectly at liberty, and yet will be for ever absolutely obedient to the divine will.

Listen again. The perfected saints will be creatures of a very peculiar form, for they will not be pure spirit, dissociated from matter. I understand yonder spirits before the throne standing in their obedience, because they have no materialism to hamper them and drag them down. Angels are spirits without material bodies, and they obey God, hearkening to his commandments; but a perfected saint is a creature in which the material is linked with the spiritual. Such are we now, and I suppose, in a measure, such shall we abide, and yet there will be no sin in us, no violation of the divine command. Man is a strange mixture. He is next akin to Deity, and yet he is brother to the worm. We are partakers of the divine nature, and the children of God; and yet as to our bodies we are linked to rocks and stones, and grosser things. Man renewed by grace touches the centre in Christ Jesus, but being still man he sweeps the circumference of creatureship, and includes within himself a summary of the whole creation. He has been called a microcosm, or a little world, and so indeed he is. Such a creature God is now perfecting. A being in whom dust and Deity each own a kindred. Such a being, purified from taint of evil, shall greatly glorify God.

Think, again, dear friends. There once stood a bright spirit in heaven, leader of the angels, but the place was too high for him, and the son of the morning fell from heaven and dragged others with him. God is making, by his grace, beings who will stand next his throne, but will remain reverently loyal for ever. They will be peers in his kingdom, but they will never be proud or ambitious. We, my brethren, though in full possession of our free agency, shall never fall from our eternal glory, but shall be faithful for ever. We shall have passed through such an experience of sin, we shall so intensely feel our indebtedness to grace, we shall so fervently love the dear Redeemer, that we shall cast our crowns at his feet, and we shall ascribe our joy to him alone, and so shall never dream of revolting from him. God is thus making beings whom it will be safe to exalt to honours so near his own: will not this be a triumph of power and goodness? Can you think of it, that you will be one of such favoured creatures, if indeed you are a believer?

These beings will have known evil. Think of that. The unfallen angels have never actually known evil, but in restored man shall be fulfilled the devil's lie made into God's truth,—"Ye shall be as gods, knowing good and evil." They shall hate evil as the burnt child dreads the fire, and they shall love righteousness because by righteousness they have been saved, and in righteousness they have been created anew. How wonderful will that creature be which has known sin, and remains a free agent, and yet will never yield to folly, but abide for ever in holiness, held by bonds of love. Oh, when I think of the destiny of a child of God, my eyes sparkle, but my tongue refuses to utter what I think. What a being art thou, O man! What art thou that God should visit thee? He has made thee "a little lower than the angels," but in Christ Jesus he has crowned thee with glory and honour, and given thee dominion over all the works of his hands, yea, in Christ he has raised thee up and made thee to sit with him in the heavenly places, far above principalities and powers, and thy time to reign and triumph for ever is hard at hand. How glorious is God in his people! God in Christ Jesus, seen in the church, who is like unto thee?

Now, the point is, that if this be the riches of God's glory in his inheritance in the saints, you may read it in another way, and say, "This is the riches of our inheritance too, for what shall we be if God is to have us for an inheritance?" Will you miss it? Will you miss it? Will you miss it? If this be a dream, I could wish to die rather than have the illusion dispelled. But it is fact, as God's word is true. Will you miss it, then? Oh, if there were crowns to be scrambled for, most men are ambitious enough to seek for one, though it might be a curse to them. If there be gold, or if there be fame, men have but to hear the chink of the metal or the blast of the trumpet, and many stir themselves to win; but here is honour, and glory, and immortality in Christ, and it is to be had for the asking; it is to be had by simply believing and trusting in Jesus Christ,—Will you not have it? Oh, false hand that is not stretched out to receive it! Oh, false heart that does not pray for it! God grant you to know what is the "riches of his inheritance in the saints," that you may seek to be a part in that inheritance and seek it now.

Now, the third "what": "What is the exceeding greatness of his power to us-ward who believe, according to the working of his mighty power, which he wrought in Christ, when he raised him from the dead, and set him at his own right hand in the heavenly places." I thought I heard somebody saying, "Woe is me! Woe is me! I hear of what man may be, I hear of what God may make of him, but woe is me; it will never come to my lot. I am so weak, so fickle, so irresolute, so frail. Woe is me; I am undone. I have no strength." Now, the third "what" is this: "that ye may know what is the exceeding greatness of his power to us-ward, who believe."

Now, learn ye this and know it—that in the conversion, preservation, and salvation of any one person God exhibits as great power as he manifested when he raised Jesus Christ from the dead and set him at his own right hand in the heavenly places. The salvation of no man in the world is by his own strength. It is by the power of God, "for we are his workmanship." This fact should greatly relieve you who are discouraged: the thing is impossible with you, but it is not impossible, or even hard, with God. He that has wrought us to the selfsame thing is God, and he is quite as able to work it in you, my dear hearer, as to work it in the apostle Paul himself. God can do all things. Now, when our Lord Jesus lay in the tomb he was dead, but God quickened him. Jesus was imprisoned in the sepulchre, and the stone at the grave's mouth was sealed and guarded; but the stone was rolled away and the guards were affrighted, and the Lord of life rose from among the dead. Every sinner is shut up in the tomb of sin by evil habit, but Christ can roll away the stone, and the sinner can come forth a living man. Our Lord continued on earth among men for several days; but, despite human enmity, no man hurt him, for he had received a life and a glory which they could not approach. The saints also abide here among men, and many seek to destroy them, but God has given them a new life, which can never be destroyed, for he hath hedged it about from all its adversaries. All the powers of darkness fought against the Lord Jesus Christ, but yet through the power of God he conquered them all. I think I see him now ascending up on high leading captivity captive in the power of God. So, my brother, you will be opposed by the powers of darkness, and by your own evil heart; but you shall conquer, for God will put forth the same power in you which he manifested in his dear Son, and you, too, shall lead captivity captive. I see the Lord Jesus entering the pearly gates and climbing to his throne, and there he sits, and none can pluck him down: and you, too, believing in Jesus, shall have the same power to tread down all your foes, your sins, your temptations, till you shall rise and sit where Jesus sits at the right hand of God. The very same power which raised Christ is waiting to raise the drunkard from his drunkenness, to raise the thief from his dishonesty, to raise the Pharisee from his self-righteousness, to raise the Sadducee from his unbelief. God has power among the sons of men, and this power he puts forth in making them to be a people that shall show forth his praise. Oh, that you knew what is the exceeding greatness of his power to us-ward who believe, because then you would fling away despair. There remains nothing for you in this case but to submit to the divine power. God will work in you; be willing to be worked upon. O, Spirit of the Lord, work in our hearers this good will. Drop yourselves like plastic clay, at the potter's feet, and he will put you on the wheel and mould you at his pleasure. Be willing, it is all he asks you; be trustful, it is all his gospel requires of you, and indeed, both will and trust he gives you. "If ye be willing and obedient ye shall eat the good of the land." Be willing to let go the sin which ruins you, be willing to learn the truth which will renew you; be willing to sit at Jesus' feet, be willing to accept a finished salvation at his hands; and all the power that is wanted to lift you from this place to the starry gates of heaven is waiting to be shed upon you. God give you to know this, and so to rest in Jesus and be saved.

II. The last word is to be upon the second head: WHY WE WISH YOU TO SEE AND KNOW ALL THIS. I have in effect been all along enforcing this second head as the sermon has progressed, and so I shall not need to detain you many minutes, except with a practical recapitulation.

We want you to know the hope of his calling that you may not neglect it, nor set anything in competition with it. I tried, as my poor words enabled me to tell you, what a hope the calling of God gives the Christian. I charge you, do not let it go. I shall, probably, never meet the most of you again, and if any shall say to you afterwards, "Well, what said the man?" I would like you to be compelled to say, "He said this—that there is a future before us of such glory that he charged us not to lose it. There are the possibilities of such intense delight for ever and ever that he besought us to ensure that delight by accepting Christ and his way of salvation."

Next we want you to believe the riches of the glory of his inheritance in the saints, that you may see where your hope lies. Your hope lies in not being your own any more, but in being the Lord's, and so realizing "the riches of the glory of God's inheritance in the saints." The saints belong to their Lord: your salvation will be found in experimentally knowing that you are not your own, because you are bought with a price; yea, in admitting at this moment that your honour and happiness is found in being the Lord's. If you are your own you will spend yourself and be ruined, but if you are Christ's he will take care of you. Oh, if I thought that I had a hair of this head that belonged to myself alone I would tear it out; but to be owned by Jesus altogether, spirit, soul, and body; to be Christ's man in the entireness of my being, this is glory, and immortality, and eternal life. Be your own, and you will be lost: be Christ's, and you are saved.

The closing thought is this. We want you to know the exceeding greatness of God's power, that you may not doubt, or despond, or despair, but come now and cast yourselves upon the incarnate God, and let him save you. Yield yourselves unto him, that the great glory of his power may be manifest in you as in the rest of his people. I am loth that you should go till you have really hidden these things in your hearts to ponder them in after days. I set bread before you, do not merely look at it, but eat a portion now and carry the rest home to eat in secret. Our preaching is often too much like a fiddler's playing. People come to see how it is done, and then they pass round the question, "What think ye of him?" Now, I do not care two straws what you think of me, but I do care a whole world what you think of Christ and of yourselves, and of your future state. I pray you forget the way in which I put things, for that may be very blundering and faulty; but if there be anything in the things themselves consider them with care. If you judge the Bible to be a fraud, and that there is no heaven to be had, then go, sport and laugh as you please, for you will only act consistently with your erroneous imagination; but if you believe God's word to be true, and that there is a glorious hope connected with the Christian's high calling, then in the name of prudence and common sense why do you not seek it? Give no sleep to your eyes nor slumber to your eyelids till you find it. I ask the Lord's people here present, and I know that there are many such in the audience to-night, to pray that this appeal may have an effect upon many in this great crowd, that they may seek the Lord at once with full purpose of heart. O Spirit of God, work it, for Jesus Christ's sake. Amen.

2
HEAVENLY GEOMETRY (1860)

"That he would grant you, according to the riches of his glory, to be strengthened with might by his Spirit in the inner man; that Christ may dwell in your hearts by faith; that ye, being rooted and grounded in love, may be able to comprehend with all saints what is the breadth, and length, and depth, and height; and to know the love of Christ, which passeth knowledge, that ye might be filled with all the fulness of God."—Eph. 3:16–19.

"No progress to any extent is to be made in the school of the cross unless you separate yourself, and give yourself wholly to this. It must be the one great business of your life, to know him and the power of his resurrection."

—

THIS divine mensuration is an art of the most desirable kind, as appears from its being the object of most earnest apostolic prayers. Paul was not content to travail in birth for souls, and to become their spiritual parent, but he afterwards exercised the functions of a nursing father, tenderly caring for the souls to whom he had been blessed, and desiring to see them growing up in the faith to the ripeness of spiritual maturity. He was parent, nurse, and tutor, in fact he became all things, as far as lay within his power, to his spiritual children. Paul's wise tenderness leads us to an assured confidence that the blessing, to pray for which he suspended his writing of so important an epistle, must have been of the very highest value. "For this cause I bow my knees unto the Father of our Lord Jesus Christ." He felt that it was desirable to the very last degree that the saints should not only know themselves to be the objects of divine favour, but should be well acquainted with its sublime qualities and perfections, which he here compares to a four-fold measurement. In this measurement may you and I be skilled. If we know nothing of mathematics, may we be well-tutored scholars in this spiritual geometry, and be able to comprehend the breadths and lengths of Jesu's precious love.

It may be well at the outset to call your attention to the previous education which the apostle desires for the saints as a preliminary to their measurement of divine love; then the mensuration itself which he desires them to practise; and lastly, the practical results which would be sure to follow from their being able to comprehend the love of Christ Jesus our Lord.

I. Like a wise and enlightened teacher, Paul desires for the saints that they should receive THAT PREVIOUS EDUCATION WHICH IS NECESSARY BEFORE THEY WILL BE ABLE TO ENTER UPON SUCH A

SCIENCE AS THE MEASUREMENT OF CHRIST'S LOVE.

When lads go to school they are not at first put to study algebra, nor are they sent out to make a trigonometrical survey of a county. The schoolmaster knows that they must have a rudimentary knowledge of arithmetic, or else to teach them algebra would be waste of time, and that they must have some acquaintance with common geometry, or it would be absurd to instruct them in surveying. He therefore begins with the elementary information, and when they have learned simpler matters they are ready for the more difficult studies. They climb the steps of the door of science, and then they are introduced to her temple. The apostle Paul does not propose that the new convert should at once be able to measure the breadth and length and depth and height of the love of Christ; he knows that this is not within the range of his infant mind; for the new-born spirit has a time of growth to go through before it can enter into the deep things of God. We must learn our alphabet at the dame's school of repentance and faith, and study the syntax of Christian holiness at the grammar-school of experience before we can enter the university of full assurance, and obtain a fellowship among those who comprehend the science of Christ crucified in its highest degree. It is not for the mere babe to compute distances or to fathom depths, this is work for men; the child will think as a child and understand as a child until instruction and years have developed his powers and fitted him for more sublime and manly thought.

If you will kindly refer to the text you will see what this previous education is which the apostle desired for the saints. It is very fully described in three parts. First. He desired that their spiritual faculties might be strengthened, for he prays that they might be "strengthened with might by the Spirit in the inner man." He does not so much intend that they may be strengthened in their mental faculties as in their spiritual capacities, to which he refers by the term inner man. The schoolmaster knows that the boy's mind must be strengthened, that his understanding must be exercised, his discernment must be developed, and his memory must be rendered capacious before he may enter upon superior studies; and the apostle knows that our spiritual faculties must undergo the same kind of development; that our faith, for instance, must be unwavering, that our love must become fervent, that our hope must be bright, that our joy must be increased, and then, but not till then, we shall be able to comprehend the length and breadth of love divine. We are to be strengthened in the inner man by the Spirit of God; and who can strengthen as he strengthens? When the divine omnipotence pours its renewing energy into our poor fainting weakness, then we grow strong indeed; when the divine intelligence enlightens our pitiful ignorance, then we grow truly wise; when the divine infinity enlarges and expands our narrow capacities to receive the truth, then are we blessedly elevated to otherwise unattainable points of blissful knowledge. Oh the blessedness of being strengthened of the Holy Ghost! How spiritually strong do we become when he infuses his might into us! But the Spirit of God works by means, and hence we may expect to have our spiritual faculties strengthened by the study of the Word, by communion with Christ, by listening to the earnest exhortations of our brethren, by experience, by prayer, and by all other hallowed exertions which grace has ordained to be the channels of communication between the heirs of the kingdom and the Comforter who abides with them for ever. Our strength to learn with must come from God the Holy Ghost. I suppose the expression "strengthened with might," is meant to refer to an eminent measure of strength. The Christian man will get to heaven should he have only strength as a grain of mustard seed. Through many difficulties the work of faith, though almost water logged, will be tugged into the harbour, for Christ is on board and secures her safety; but it is not desirable that we should thus struggle into eternal life; it is far more to be hoped that our young faculties may come to healthy and vigorous manhood, so that, to return to our former metaphor, our vessel, stanch and in good trim, with her sails well filled, and her flags flying right gallantly, having outridden every storm, may have an abundant entrance into the desired haven. Brethren, I trust you are not among those who think it quite enough to be barely alive unto God; I trust that you wish to be not only babes in the family, but young men and fathers in the household; and that you even aspire to be strengthened by the Holy Ghost with might, that you may become powerful men, men able to enter into the soul and marrow of divine things, and to discern between things that differ. I would have you not mere milk-fed infants, but men able to crack the nuts of the gospel, and to digest the strong meat, because by reason of years you have had all your senses exercised. Why should we for ever be obliged to lay again the foundations? Why not press onward and upward in heavenly attainments as men do in human learning? Why must our heads always wear the dunce's cap, and our backs smart with the fool's rod? The Holy Spirit works in us to this very end that we may be no more mere children, but well-taught men of God. Oh grieve him not, but be willing to be taught! This was the object of the apostle's prayers, and of our loving anxieties. Be reminded, beloved, that none of you will be able to comprehend the mensuration of the love of Christ, unless first of all the Holy Ghost our Instructor shall have baptized your spiritual powers with his sacred influences, and so have strengthened you with might in that refined and new created part of your being which is called the inner man, because it is your truest, most precious, most secret, most vital, most essential self.

A second part of this preliminary education is mentioned by our apostle in the next sentence,—"That Christ may dwell in your hearts by faith." He desires that the object of study may be evermore before them. A good tutor not only wishes his scholar may have a disciplined mind able to grapple with the subject, but he endeavours to keep the subject always before him; for in order to attain to any proficiency in a science the mind must be abstracted from all other thoughts, and continually exercised with the chosen theme. You will never find a man pre-eminent in astronomy unless astronomy has become the lord of mind, and holds a sway over his mind even in his dreams. The anatomist must be bound to nerves, and bones, and blood vessels, as the galley slave is bound to the oar, or he will never master his subject. The botanist must be enamoured of every flower, and wedded to every plant, or the fields will utterly baffle him. "Through desire a man, having separated himself, seeketh and intermeddleth with all wisdom." Solomon knew what he wrote when he said, "Separated himself," for without separation or abstraction there can be no progress. Now, the apostle desires that we who are believers, our faculties being strengthened, may have the person of Jesus constantly before us to inflame our love, and so increase our knowledge. See how near he would have Jesus to be! "That Christ may dwell in your hearts by faith." Yon cannot get a subject closer to you than to have it on the inner side of the eyes; that is to say, in the heart itself. The astronomer cannot always see the stars because they are far away, and outside of him; but our star shines in the heaven of our hearts evermore. The botanist must find his flowers in their seasons, but our plant of renown blooms in our souls all the year round. We carry the instruments of our saintly art, and the object of our devout contemplation within ourselves. As a scholar carries in his pocket a small edition of his favourite classic, so do we carry Christ in our hearts; what if I say we bear about with us a heart edition of the Liber Crucis, the Book of the Cross. Renewed hearts need no other library than themselves, for Jesus in our inmost spirits is library enough. If we knew more fully by experience the meaning of "Christ in you the hope of glory," our heaven-taught affections, which are the best part of our inner man, might be continually exercised upon the person, the work, and the love of our dear Redeemer. "That Christ may dwell in your hearts." Brothers and sisters, it will be to small profit that we shall talk to you about the breadth, and length, and depth, and height, of the love of Christ unless there be in your soul a devout longing ambition to set the Lord Jesus always before you, as the frequent, if not, the constant

31

subject of your meditations. No progress to any extent is to be made in the school of the cross unless you separate yourself, and give yourself wholly to this. It must be the one great business of your life, to know him and the power of his resurrection. I would to God that we were all entered as diligent scholars in Jesus' college, students of Corpus Christi, or the body of Christ, resolved to attain unto a good degree in the learning of the cross, a learning which angels desire to understand; but to do this the heart must be full of Jesus, welling up with his love, flaming with it, overrunning with it; and hence the apostle prays, "that Christ may dwell in your hearts." Observe the words, "that he may dwell;" not that he may call upon you sometimes, as a casual visitor enters into a house and tarries for a night, but that he may dwell, that Christ may take up his abode in your hearts, that the Lord Jesus may become the Lord and tenant of your inmost being, never more to go out, but to dwell there world without end. Observe too, the words—that he may dwell in your hearts, that best room of the house of manhood; not in your thoughts alone, but in your affections; not merely have him in your minds, but have him in your loves. Paul wants you to have a love to Christ of a most abiding character, not a love that flames up under an earnest sermon, and then dies out into the darkness of a few embers, but a constant flame, the abiding of Jesu's love in your hearts, both day and night, like the flame upon the altar which never went out. This cannot be accomplished except by faith. Faith must be strong, or love will not be fervent; the root of the flower must be healthy, or we cannot expect the bloom to be sweet. Faith is the lily's root, and love is the lily's bloom. Now Jesus cannot be in your heart's love except you have a firm hold of him by your heart's faith; and, therefore, he prays that you may always trust Christ, that you may always love him. Thus, brethren, the Lord Jesus being constantly brought under your heart's attention, you are likely to be able to comprehend the measurement of his love, which it would otherwise be impossible for you to do.

The apostle prays further that they may have practical exercise in the art of holy love; "that ye being rooted and grounded in love." Every experienced tutor knows that it is greatly helpful to the student to exercise him in his chosen pursuit upon some lower and inferior branch of it, so as to lead him gradually to the higher points of it. If for instance, he means him to understand the surveying of estates, he bids him measure a field containing an acre or two. If he means him to map out a country, he sets him first to make a plan of a neighbouring field or a farm. The apostle acts upon the same method. "That ye, being rooted and grounded in love, may be able to comprehend the breadth and length of the love of Christ." Having the love of Jesus in you, possessed with love to Christ, you will be practised in the exercise of love, and so will understand the love which filled the Saviour. You will learn to do business upon the greater waters of the Redeemer's infinite love to his people as you sail upon the stream of your love to him.

Two expressions are used:—"rooted," like a living tree which lays hold upon the soil, twists itself round the rocks, and cannot be upturned:—"grounded," like a building which has been settled, as a whole, and will never show any cracks or flaws in the future through failures in the foundation. The apostle wishes us to be rooted and grounded in love, a vital union being established between our souls and Jesus, so that we love him because he first loved us; and also a fiducial union, or a union of trust, by which we rest upon Jesus as the stones of a wall are settled upon the foundation. He would have us thus by love and by faith to be knit to Christ, and to be firm, and fast, and fixed, and immoveable in our loving attachment to him.

My dear brothers and sisters, you cannot know Christ's love to you, to any great extent, except you thus love him. You must love, or you cannot comprehend love. A man who has never felt benevolence towards his fellow creatures—and there are some such monsters—sneers and laughs at those who can give their money to the poor or to the sick. He thinks such persons fools at least, if not absolutely mad. "Ah," said one, "I know how to make money," and then he added significantly, clenching his fist, "and I know what some people do not know; I know how to take care of it too." There are some benevolent people who do not know how to take care of it in that sense, but they know how to do good with it, and such people will never be comprehended by the mean money-grubbing wretch who pollutes the earth he lives upon. As though he were a very Solomon, and benevolent men were idiots, he mutters conceitedly, "Well, I cannot understand it; it is stupidity to give away your hard-earned money." Of course it is to him; he cannot comprehend it. So the love of Jesus Christ cannot be comprehended by a man who does not love. If you have no love to souls, you will not understand why Jesus wept over Jerusalem; it will puzzle you mightily; yon will look to Matthew Henry, and Scott, and Gill, and be more puzzled still; but if you love the souls of men, you will find no difficulty in the passage at all, for you will weep over sinners too. If you do not love the saints, you will wonder how Jesus can love them; but when you have once felt an unselfish Christ-like love to your fellow men, the riddle will be answered. He who circumnavigated the world began by sailing upon brooks and mill-ponds, and he who would measure the breadths and lengths of Jesu's love must feel his own soul filled with affection for his Lord.

Paul would have us, then, with developed faculties, with the subject in our hearts, and with an exercise of love on our part, prepared to enter upon the science. My brethren, when I consider what a science it is, the science of the love of Christ, the most masterly of all knowledge, too deep for the archangel's intellect, the wonder of all the hosts of heaven,—when I consider that the greatest human minds have confessed themselves to be altogether lost in the contemplation, and have had to say, "Oh the depths! Oh the depths!" I do not wonder at all that the apostle, instead of praying for us that we might immediately enter upon the study of it, first prays that we may be gratified to learn it; for as some sciences, if taught to an illiterate man, would be only taught in their letter, but could not be learnt in their spirit for want of capacity to receive them, so the love of Jesus Christ in its length, and breadth, and depth, and height, if it could be taught in the letter of it to an untrained believer, would be in a great measure lost upon him; he would not be deriving true knowledge therefrom; he would observe the letter, but the inward spirit he would not be able to understand. Beloved, if you are to win the precious attainment of the knowledge of Christ's love in its depth and breadth, you must pray that God would strengthen your spiritual powers, you must plead that Jesus may abide in your souls, and that your love to him may become vigorous and all absorbing, for thus only can you drink deeply into the unutterable and infinite love of Jesus.

II. We now come to Consider more closely the SCIENCE OF HEAVENLY MENSURATION ITSELF.

According to the text, we have a solid body to deal with, for we are to measure its breadth and length, and depth, and height. This cubical measurement—for it lieth foursquare, like the new Jerusalem—proves the reality of the body to be measured. Alas, to a great many religious people the love of Jesus is not a solid substantial thing at all—it is a beautiful fiction, a sentimental belief, a formal theory, but to Paul it was a real, substantial, measurable fact; he had considered it this way, and that way, and the other way, and it was evidently real to him, whatever it might be to others. No one knows the love of Christ at all if he does not know it to be real, and no one has felt it in his soul at all unless it becomes so real as to constrain him and move him into actual activity. We have a word which we sometimes use in a sense which I believe is not correct according to the dictionary; I mean the word "realise:" that word has been forced into the language of Christian experience, and can never be forced out again; we must realise, or make real to our hearts the love of Christ. That is just what I think the apostle did—he made real to himself the love of his Master and Lord. It was not to him a surface theory, which might have breadth, but could not have depth; or a mere narrow statement with length, but no breadth; it was a thing as firm and solid as anything in the world. It is true the love of Jesus is not material and earthly so as to be seen and handled, but it is even more substantial than if it were a thing to be seen, for the things which are seen are temporal, and the things which are not seen are eternal. To the carnal man the visible is real, and the invisible a mere dream; but to the spiritual man things are reversed, the visible is the shadow and the invisible the substance. May you be such men, dear friends, all of you!

The apostle desires that when the love of Christ becomes to us a solid reality we may have close communion with it. You may measure the breadth and length of a thing at a great distance, but you cannot very well measure its depth without drawing near to it. What a holy familiarity with Jesus do the words imply when we come to measurements of all kinds! What condescension is this which allows the sacred heart to be fathomed like a sea, and to be measured as a field! Shall the infinite thus bow itself to man? Shall man refuse to commune with such condescending love? Should it not be our deep desire to obtain and to retain the most intimate acquaintance with the thrice blessed love of Jesus, so as not only to measure it in one form, but in all forms, that in every way in which the love of Christ may be regarded, from above or from below, we may be well acquainted with it. We should know the inmost secrets of the Redeemer's love; its doings and sacrifices which are the apparent part of it—its breadth, its counsels and its plans—its depth, the secret part of it—its length, its endurance and patience—its height, its triumphs and glories. We would know all that is knowable, for when we know all that has been learned by mortals, there is still a something that is beyond our view, and hence the apostle adds, "to know the love of Christ, which passeth knowledge."

Let me come to the very words of our text, and point out to you their order. The first object of the Christian's knowledge should be the breadth of the Saviour's love. I know a certain school of Christians who have need to study this point, for they have a very narrow idea of the Lord's loving-kindness. They cannot be brought by any means to conceive of it as being broad; to them it is no wider than a razor's edge. They conceive of divine love as a very narrow stream, they have never seen it to be a mighty, flowing, abounding, and rejoicing river, such as it really is. The breadth of Christ's love, dear friends, we are told in Scripture, is such that it extends to all ranks and races of mankind—not to the Jew only, but also to the Gentile. The love of Jesus Christ does not surround our favoured island alone, but like the ocean it washes every shore. The love of Jesus Christ has been extended to kings upon their thrones, but with equal and more frequent bounty to the slaves in their dungeons. In some respects the love of Jesus comes to every man, for there is not a man or woman born who does not owe something to the benevolence of God through the love of Jesus. The respite which keeps the sinner out of hell is no doubt the result of that love which said, "Spare it yet a little longer, till I dig about it and dung it, and if it bring forth fruit, well." Beloved, the benevolent love of Jesus is more extended than the lines of his electing love; for we hear him saying, "O Jerusalem, Jerusalem, which killest the prophets, and stonest them that are sent unto thee; how often would I have gathered thy children together, as a hen doth gather her brood under her wings, and ye would not" That is not the love which beams resplendently upon his chosen, but it is true love for all that; pitying and benevolent love which revealed itself in honest tears of grief. I would not have you omit this view of the subject when you are measuring its breadth, although we still feel that in its utmost depth and fulness that love flows only to his people. Beloved, consider the breadth of special love, we are very apt to conceive the number of God's elect to be but few. Who told us that? When the Saviour was asked, "Lord, are there few that shall be saved?" he never answered that question, but he said, "Strive to enter into the strait gate;" as though he had said, "Whether there be many or not, do you strive to the utmost to enter in." I hope that the multitude of the chosen will far exceed the number of the lost. It has always seemed to me that if in all things Christ will have the pre-eminence, he will not suffer the powers of darkness to drag away the major part of the human race; but on the contrary, a multitude that no man can number, so many as the stars in heaven for multitude, and like the sands upon the sea-shore innumerable, shall be the fruit of his suffering, which shall make him to see of the travail of his soul, and to be satisfied. It is well to have as broad ideas of the love of Christ as Scripture will permit us, and there I trust we shall be content to stay. But, brethren, we get the best idea of the breadth of Christ's love, when we behold it flowing to our lost and guilty selves: I never thought it so broad a stream till I found that it reached to me, even to me. I feared that I was far away from its blessed margin, but the river swelled and overflowed its banks until at last it washed me, even me.

How broad it must have been to have reached to some here present, who had wandered into the plains of sin, and had followed after their own wanton devices, but yet the breadth of the river embraced even them. You may measure the breadth of it by the sins which it covers. When a river is overflowing, you tell how broad it must be by the little hillocks and the tree tops which you can see in it. You may see how broad is the love of Christ, that it reaches to such offences as these:—it reaches to theft, to drunkenness, to blasphemy, to fornication, to adultery, to murder. The Saviour's measurement of it is this, "All manner of sin and of blasphemy shall be forgiven unto men." There is a bound, it stops at one sin which is unto death, but of that we know nothing, and I trust we never may; but with that one exception broad as sin is, so broad is this mighty love of Christ which covers it all.

Do you not think, however, that we most of us fail to see the breadth of Christ's love in matters of providence? You know what is meant by the breadth of a man's mind, the breadth of his thought, when he can consider a great many subjects at once, when he has the ability to accomplish many designs and many purposes with one stroke. Now, the breadth of the Saviour's love is just this: there is no part of his people's interests which he does not consider, and there is nothing which concerns their welfare which is not important to him. Not merely does he think of you, believer, as an immortal being, but as a mortal being too. Do not deny it or doubt it; the very hairs of your head are all numbered. There is nothing that concerns his beloved that is unimportant to our Lord. "The steps of a good man are ordered by the Lord, and he delighteth in his way." It were a sad thing for us if this river of love did not cover all our concerns, for what mischief might be wrought for us in that part of our business which did not come under our gracious Lord's inspection! Oh! believer, rest assured that the heart of Jesus concerns itself about your meaner affairs; your buying and selling he cares for, your counter and counting-house, your ships and your carts and your horses, and your barley, and your wheat, and your hay, and your straw; your children, your little ones, and everything which concerns you concerns him also. The breadth of his tender love is such that you may go to him in all matters; for in all your afflictions he is afflicted, and like as a father pitieth his children, so doth he pity you.

This invites us to look at the breadth of the Saviour's love under a still greater aspect. All the concerns of all his saints that have ever lived or ever shall live, are all borne upon the broad bosom of the Son of God. Oh what a heart his is, that doth not merely comprehend the persons of his people, but comprehends the diverse and innumerable concerns of all those persons! Alexander, it is said, knew the names of his soldiers, but Alexander could not think of every soldier in every tent, and of all the business of every soldier; but this the love of Christ does, he thinks of all the cares and all the troubles and all the joys present and to come of every blood-bought one. Now see, dear friend, if thou canst measure the breadth of the love of Christ. Thou hast a task before thee which thou wilt not yet accomplish, and if thou couldst there would still remain another breadth, namely, that breadth measured by the boons which he brings. Think of what he has brought you! He has brought you justification, ay! adoption, sanctification, eternal life. The riches of his goodness are unsearchable, you shall never be able to tell them out or even conceive them. Oh the breadth of the love of Christ!

And yet you see this is merely a beginning because the breadth and measurement is but surface work. This is for you youngsters to think about, but yet I wish some of the elder Christians would. Some of them seem to be so taken up with the height and length that they deny the breadth, and you would think from hearing them preach that Christ came into the world to save half-a-dozen, and that they were five of them; at least that nobody else could go to heaven except such as they were, who swore by their Shibboleth and agreed in every jot and tittle with their creed. Out on their narrowness! There will be more in heaven than we expect to see there by a long way; and there will be some there with whom we had very little comfortable fellowship on earth who had fellowship with Christ, and who are therefore taken to dwell with him for ever.

The next object of study is the length of Christ's love. It has been well observed, that if Christ had thought upon his people for ten minutes it would have been a wonderful condescension; in fact it would have been a thing to sing of in heaven that Christ Jesus did once think upon us, because we are not worthy of a minute of God's thoughts. Now just try if you can grasp the thought, he has thought upon his people as long as he has existed. Is it not eternal love, and what is longer than that? "I have loved thee with an everlasting love." Coeval then with Deity itself is the love of Deity towards its chosen ones. God did love us in his Son long before the world began. If an angel were to start from to-day with the design of finding out when God's love began he would doubtless fly on till he lingered at the cross. "Here," he would say, "here is the fountain, here is the source of it all." But he would be reminded that "God so loved the world that he gave his only begotten Son." Then there was a love before the giving of his Son. He would fly onward till he paused at Isaiah's day and heard of God's lore in the prophecy that the Son of man should bear the iniquity of his people. He would say, "Surely it begins here!" But saints would remind him of yet older words of comfort, and he would fly on till he stopped outside of the garden of Eden and heard the Lord say, "The seed of the woman shall bruise the serpent's head." "Surely," saith he, "it began here." But divinely instructed he would go back yet further, even to the eternal councils where first of all salvation was planned and contrived in the cabinets of wisdom before the world was. He would have to go back, back, back, till creation had vanished, till there remained not a shred of existence except the absolute self-existent Deity, and then in the Eternal Mind he would see thoughts of love toward a people to be formed for himself. This knowledge of the length of love does not always come to Christians early in their history. Some of my dear brethren know the breadth of Christ's love right well, but they seem as if they never would learn its length. Some of our Arminian friends know a great deal about the breadth of it, and can preach very sweetly upon it too, and I thank God they can, for they are the means of bringing in many converts who might not be brought in if it were not for their broad preaching. Yes, dear brethren, it may be as broad as you like, but it must be long too. You must not preach a love that begins when you begin, but a love which is beforehand with you—a causeless love which is the cause and not the effect of your love—a love which knows no beginning, but is ancient as the throne of Deity.

This love is not only without beginning but it is without pause. There is never a moment when Jesus ceases to love his people. The love of Jesus knows nothing of suspended animation. There are some rivers in Australia which lose themselves, and for miles along their bed you find nothing but dry stones at certain seasons of the year. It is never so with the love of Christ: it is long, and without a break from beginning to end; it is a chain without a single broken or feeble link. The love of Jesus possesses an eternal existence in which there is not a single intermission, nor even a sign of failure or hint of an end. Here let us rejoice without trembling. "Having loved his own which were in the world, he loved them to the end." We lean our heads upon this pillow and we sleep right sweetly there,—"He which hath begun a good work in you will perform it until the day of Jesus Christ." "For the gifts and calling of God are without repentance." "He saith, I am God, I change not, therefore ye sons of Jacob are not consumed." "Jesus Christ, the same yesterday, to-day, and for ever." "For whom he did foreknow, he also did predestinate to be conformed to the image of his Son, that he might be the firstborn among many brethren. Moreover whom he did predestinate, them he also called; and whom he called, them he also justified; and whom he justified, them he also glorified." There are no ifs and buts in this circle of grace. All is certain as the throne of God. Our conquering

Captain shall bring many sons to glory, and his shall be the praise. Dear friends, we studiously consider the length of this love of Christ, but I am persuaded, study it as we may, we shall never completely grasp it. It is so long that your old age cannot wear it out, so long that your continual tribulations cannot exhaust it, your successive temptations shall not drain it dry: like eternity itself it knows no bounds.

My time has fled, and I am only in the centre of my subject, and therefore the rest of the discourse must be in brief hints and hurried sentences. The depth of the love of Jesus! Consider it as stooping to look upon such an insignificant creature as man! View the depth of that love in receiving such sinful creatures into his embrace! What a depth is seen when the Lord Jesus Christ selects some guilty wretch who has openly broken the laws of his country, and subjected himself to punishment from his fellowmen, and yet the Lord Jesus freely pardons him when he repents of sin, and receives him into his heart's love. The depth of this river of love is best seen however in the fact that Jesus became a man, Deity became incarnate! the Lord of angels slept upon a woman's breast. Nor is this enough. Being a man, he bears our sorrows, goes through the world weary, and poor, and patient; a man of sorrows, and acquainted with grief. Nor is this all, he bears our sins. The iniquities of his people, like a huge load, are laid upon his shoulders, and he stands as their substitute. Even yet it is not enough, for he bears our punishment, and on the bloody tree he bows his head, and is obedient even unto death. Hell's waves rolled over him, the eternal wrath of God spent itself upon his blessed head; he was made lower than the angels are, but he stooped lower still, till he called himself a worm and no man. Oh the depth of the agony of Jesus smarting for sin! O sinner! you cannot have gone too deep for Christ's love to reach you. O backslider! you cannot have sinned too foully for forgiveness. Thou who hast gone beyond conception in sin, thou who hast practised the foulest and most devilish of sins, the depth of Christ's love is still deeper, and he is able to save even to the uttermost.

Think next of the height of the Master's love. You see it is put last, as the highest point of learning. There are some who have advanced as far as to understand somewhat of the depths, who do not know the full dignity and glory of an heir of heaven, and have felt but little of the power of his ascension. Why, the love of Jesus, even in this present life, is a height unspeakable, for has it not lifted us up to become sons of God? "And if children, then heirs, heirs of God, and joint heirs with Christ." It has given us an earnest of the inheritance, it has made us anticipate the hour when we shall dwell with the angels of light; it tells us that our conversation is in heaven, and that our life is hid with Christ in God. Yet, brethren, the height of this love will be best seen in a future state. You shall be borne up to dwell with Christ in the clouds when the world is in a blaze, and when the judgment is passed you shall be carried by angels' wings up to the seventh heaven where God dwelleth. Oh the breadth, the length, the depth, the height! To sum up what we have said in four words. For breadth the love of Jesus is immensity, for length it is eternity, for depth it is immeasurability, and for height it is infinity. O Christian, may the Holy Spirit instruct you in these great things!

III. Lastly, two or three words. If it shall be our privilege to study this science and to master it, albeit it will still be over and above us, for it passeth all knowledge, there will flow the following PRACTICAL RESULTS. We shall be filled with all the fulness of God.

Brethren, do try and get hold of this marvellous expression when you are alone in meditation. Set it before you as a great mystery to be dived into. "Filled with all the fulness of God," what can it meat? Is it to have God within you; God dwelling in your inmost spirit? It is this, but more. "Filled with Gods" to hold as much of God; as your nature can hold; what a thought! "Filled with God," even this is not all. "Filled with the fulness of God." The fulness of his love and grace, and power, and holiness can come to dwell in you; but this is not all that the verse speaks of, it is written, "filled with all the fulness of God." What a transcendent expression! Here we have not only an indwelling God, but that God in the utmost fulness of his Godhead filling and overflowing the whole soul with his fulness. I cannot help borrowing an illustration from a friend who took up a bottle by the seashore, filled it full of sea-water, corked it down, and then threw it into the sea. "Now," said he, "there it is, there is the sea in the bottle, and there is the bottle in the sea." It is full to fulness, and then in a still greater fulness. There is my soul with God in it, and my soul in God; the fulness of God in me as much as I can hold, and then myself in the fulness of God. The illustration gives one as much of the text as one knows how to convey; ourselves swallowed up in the all-absorbing abyss of the love of God, and that same love of God flowing into all the parts and powers of our soul till we are as full of God as man can hold. Then shall we show that love in our lives, in our prayers, in our preaching, in everything that we do; we shall manifest not only that we have been with Jesus, but that we have Jesus dwelling in us, filling us right full with his loving, sanctifying, elevating presence.

Beloved, if we shall reach the point indicated in the text, we shall then begin to imitate the love of God in its four aspects. I am sure if we shall ever learn the breadth of Christ's love our love will grow broad: we shall no longer confine our love to our own church, but shall care for all the churches of God; we shall feel an affection not only for Christians of our own name, but to Christians of all names. Then our love will gain length also. We shall love Christ so that we cannot leave off loving him. We shall persevere in love, we shall abide in his love as he abides in it. We shall constantly have the flame of our love going up to heaven. And then our love will acquire depth. We shall be humbled on account of our own sinfulness, we shall sink lower and lower in our own esteem, and our love will become deeper and more grounded as it descends more fully into the core of our nature. And then love will climb the heights. We shall forget the world and the cares thereof; we shall become Christians who lie no longer among the pots, but who have received the wings of a dove covered with silver, and her feathers with yellow gold. We shall attain to such a height in our love, that we shall scale the mountain tops of the promises, and with our foreheads bathed in the sunlight shall look down upon the world that still lieth in darkness, and rejoice that we are made heirs of light; till our love mounting to heaven shall there be in its height as we appear before the great white throne, and cast our crowns with many a song before him who loved us, with a breadth, and length, and depth, and height of love that even in heaven shall surpass all measurement. God bless you, dear friends, with this love, for Christ's sake. Amen.

SPIRITUAL KNOWLEDGE AND ITS PRACTICAL RESULTS (1883)

"For this cause we also, since the day we heard it, do not cease to pray for you, and to desire that ye might be filled with the knowledge of his will in all wisdom and spiritual understanding; that ye might walk worthy of the Lord unto all pleasing, being fruitful in every good work, and increasing in the knowledge of God."—Colossians 1:9,10.

"Oh, to be filled with the knowledge of the Lord's will till you know what sanctification means, and exhibit it in your daily life."

—

FOR the church that was at Colosse Paul gave hearty thanks to God for many most important blessings, especially for their faith, their love, and their hope. It would be a very useful exercise to our hearts if we would often give thanks to God for the gifts and graces which we discover in our Christian brethren. I am afraid we are more inclined to spy out their faults, and to suppose that we deplore them, than we are to discern the work of the Holy Spirit in them, and from the bottom of our hearts to give thanks to God for them. Paul felt encouraged by what he saw in the Colossian believers to pray to God to enrich them yet further. It should be our desire that our best brethren should be better, and that those who are most like Jesus should be still more completely conformed to his image. We cannot more wisely show our love to our friends than by first acknowledging the grace which is in them, and then by praying that God may give them more. Paul, as with an eagle eye, surveyed the church at Colosse, which he loved so well, and he noted that it was somewhat lacking in knowledge. The Colossian brotherhood differed considerably from the church at Corinth, which abounded in talent, and was enriched with all knowledge. The Colossians had fewer gifted brethren among them who could act as teachers, and, though this was no fault of theirs, it impoverished them in the matter of knowledge, and as Paul would not have them come behind in any desirable attainment, he therefore prayed for them that they might be filled with knowledge in all wisdom and spiritual understanding. If you read this epistle through, you will observe that Paul frequently alludes to knowledge and wisdom. To the point in which he judged the church to be deficient he turned his prayerful attention. He would not have them ignorant. He knew that spiritual ignorance is the constant source of error, instability, and sorrow; and therefore he desired that they might be soundly taught in the things of God. Not that they were destitute of saving knowledge already, for he says in the sixth verse that they "knew the grace of God in truth," and that they had brought forth fruits meet for salvation; but saving knowledge, though it be the most essential attainment, is not the only knowledge which a Christian should seek after. He longs to be useful as well as to be safe. Being himself delivered out of darkness he strives to bring others into the marvellous light of grace. Paul would have his brethren thoroughly furnished for sacred service, knowing the will of the Lord themselves, and able to teach others. He desired for them that they might possess comforting knowledge, strengthening knowledge, edifying knowledge, sanctifying knowledge, directing knowledge; so that they might be ready for all the trials, duties, and labours of life.

Upon this subject I am led to make four observations, and to enlarge upon each of them. May the Holy Spirit by this discourse build us up in the knowledge of God.

I. My first subject is THE GREAT VALUE OF INTERCESSORY PRAYER; for as soon as Paul felt his heart burning with love to the saints at Colosse, and had heard of the work of the Spirit among them, he began to show his love by lifting up his heart in prayer for them. He did that for them which he knew would bless them.

Notice, that intercessory prayer is a very important part of the work of Christians for one another. We are not sent into the world to live unto ourselves, but we are members of one body, and each member is expected to contribute to the health and the comfort of the whole. It is true we cannot all preach, but we can all pray; we cannot all distribute alms from our substance, but we can all offer prayer from our hearts. In temporal things we may not be able to enrich the church for lack of substance; but if we fail to bless the church by our prayers it will be for lack of grace. Whatever you fail in, dearly beloved,—and I pray that you may in nothing come behind,—yet do not fail in prayer for all the saints, that every blessing may abound towards them.

Intercessory prayer is to be esteemed as an invaluable proof of love, and as the creator of more love. The man who will truly pray for me will certainly forgive me readily if I offend him; he will relieve me if I am in necessity; and he will be prepared to assist me if I am engaged in a service too hard for me. Give us your earnest prayers, and we know that we live in your hearts. How sweet it is to be permitted thus to manifest our love to one another! When our hand is palsied we can still pray; when our eye grows dim we can see to pray; when by sickness we are altogether laid aside we can still pray; and when we meet with cases in which we are unable to help, and yet are moved with sympathy for a brother, our sympathy can always find one open channel, for we can pray, and by prayer call in the aid of one whose help is effectual. Therefore, by your love to your Lord, and to all those who are in him, I beseech you abound in intercessory prayer, as the apostle did.

Intercessory prayer, again, is most valuable, because it is an infallible means of obtaining the blessings which we desire for our friends. It is not in vain that we ask, for it is written, "Everyone that asketh receiveth." It is not in vain that we intercede for others, for the Lord delights to answer such petitions. The unselfish devotion which pleads as eagerly for others as for itself is so pleasing to the Lord that he puts great honour upon it. If we desire any blessing for our friends our best course is to pray: even if we would have them to be filled with knowledge in all wisdom our safest course is to pray that it may be so. Of course, we must not forget to instruct them and to aid them in their own studies as far as lieth in our power, for every honest prayer supposes the use of all proper means; but the instruction which we offer will be of no service unless we first bring down the blessing of God upon it, that thereby our friends may be made willing to learn, and may receive the truth not as the word of man, but as from the Lord himself. None but spiritual teaching will nourish spiritual life. The Holy Ghost must teach divine truth to the heart, or it will never be truly known. Whatsoever thou wisely desirest for thy friend go about to get it for him, but hasten first to the throne of grace. If thou wouldst have thy friend converted, if thou wouldst have him strengthened, if thou wouldst have him taught of God, if thou wouldst have him quickened to a nobler life, and elevated to a higher consecration, do him this great service—take his case before the Lord in prayer; and in so doing thou hast gone the wisest way to work to enrich him.

Note, brethren, for I am keeping to my text closely, that such intercessory prayer will be all the more valuable if it is our immediate resort. The apostle says, "Since the day we heard it, we do not cease to pray for you." He began to pray at once. Whenever you perceive the work of the Spirit in any heart, pray at once, that the holy change may proceed with power. Whenever you discover any lack in a brother begin on the day you hear of it to pray that his lack may be supplied. There should be no delaying of prayer. "He gives twice who gives quickly" is a human proverb, but I believe that when we pray speedily we shall often find that God in answering quickly gives us a double blessing. Usually he shall win worldly riches who is the most diligent in the pursuit of them, and assuredly he shall be richest towards God who is most diligent in supplication. Linger not a minute, speed thee to the mercy-seat. Now is the accepted time; the Lord waits to be gracious to thee. The Lord indicates to thee what thy prayer shall be by the news which thou hast just heard of thy friend; therefore, bring his case at once before the throne of grace. Divine providence has brought the needful subject for prayer under thy notice; therefore, this day begin to pray about it.

Our prayers will be all the more valuable if they are incessant as well as immediate. "We cease not," said Paul, "to pray for you since the day we heard it." "Oh," says one, "was Paul always praying for the Colossians from the day he heard of their welfare? It may have been months and years; did he never cease to pray?" I answer, he was always praying for them in the sense which he explains: he adds, "and to desire." Now, desire is the essence of prayer; in fact, desire is the kernel of prayer, and the vocal expressions which we call by the name of prayer are often but its shell; inward desire is the life, the heart, the reality of prayer. Though you cannot always be speaking in prayer, you can always be desiring in prayer. The miser is always desiring riches, though he is not always talking about his gold and silver; and the man who loves his fellow-men, and desires their profit, is really always praying for their benefit, though he is not always lifting up his voice in supplication. "Since the day we heard it," saith Paul, "we do not cease to pray for you." The act of prayer is blessed, the habit of prayer is more blessed, but the spirit of prayer is the most blessed of all; and it is this that we can continue for months and years. The act of prayer must, from force of circumstances, be sometimes stayed; but the habit of prayer should be fixed and unvarying; and the spirit of prayer, which is fervent desire, should be perpetual and abiding. We can hardly realize the value to the church and to the world of that intercessory prayer which ceases not day nor night, but without fail ascends before the Lord from the whole company of the faithful, as the incense ascended from the altar.

Dear friends, our intercessory prayer will be all the more precious if it is an intense expression unto God. I suppose that by the use of the word "desire" here, the apostle not only explains how he continued to pray, but in what manner he prayed—with "desire." Remember how our Lord puts it—"with desire have I desired to eat this passover with you before I surfer." I wish we could always say "with desire have I desired in prayer. I did not repeat a merely complimentary benediction upon my friends, but I pleaded for them as for my life; I importuned with God; I offered an effectual inwrought prayer, which rose from the depths of my heart to the heights of heaven, and obtained an audience with God." Fervency is a great essential for victorious prayer. God grant us to be importunate, for then we shall be invincible.

One more observation, and I have done with this. Intercessory prayer is increased in value when it is not from one person alone, but is offered in intimate union with other saints. Paul says, "We also," not "I only," but

"We also, since the day we heard it, cease not." If two of you agree as touching anything concerning the kingdom, you have the blessing secured to you by a special promise of God. Remember how Abraham prayed for the cities of the plain, but succeeded not until. Lot also added his supplication for Zoar. Then the little city was spared. I compare Abraham's intercession to a ton weight of prayer, and poor Lot's I can hardly reckon to have been more than half an ounce, but still that half ounce turned the scale. So here is Paul, and with him is youthful Timothy, who, compared with Paul, is inconsiderable; yet. Paul's prayer is all the more effectual because Timothy's prayer is joined with it. Our Lord sent out his servants by two and two, and it is well when they come back to him in prayer two and two. I commend to you, brethren and sisters, the habit of frequent prayer together. When a Christian friend drops in, his visit will perhaps end in mere talk unless you secure its spiritual profit by at least a few minutes spent in united prayer. I frequently during the day, when a friend comes in upon the Master's business, say, "Let us pray before you go," and I always find the request is welcomed. Such prayers do not occupy much time, and if they did, it might be well spent; but such united supplications oil the wheels of life's heavy wain, and cause it to move with less of that creaking which we too often hear. "I alone" is certainly a good word in prayer; but "we also" is a better one. Let us link hands and intercede for our brethren and the whole church of God.

Thus have I expatiated upon the excellences which increase the value of intercessory prayer. Use much this heavenly art. It is effectual for ten thousand ends. It turneth every way to bless the church. Brethren, pray for us, pray for all saints, pray for all sinners, and by so doing you will be the benefactors of your age.

II. Our second observation from the text is this—we learn here THE PRECIOUSNESS OF SPIRITUAL KNOWLEDGE; for all this earnest, ceaseless prayer is offered for this end, "That ye might be filled with the knowledge of his will in all wisdom and spiritual understanding." Here let us speak of the usefulness and blessedness of that spiritual knowledge for which the apostle and his friend cried incessantly unto the Lord.

First, consider the men for whom this knowledge is desired. They are saints and faithful brethren, of whom we read that they "knew the grace of God in truth," and were "bringing forth fruit" unto God. For those who know the Lord already we must not cease to pray. They are not beyond the need of our prayers while they are in this life. We may pray for those who know nothing of the Lord, that he would open their blind eyes; but even those who have been taught of God already are in need of our supplications that they may learn yet more. We have great encouragement to pray that they may be filled with all knowledge, since the Lord has already done so much for them. We dare not say in this case that a little knowledge is a dangerous thing, for a little knowledge of the things of God may suffice to save the soul; but more knowledge is a most desirable thing for those who have that little knowledge. Pray therefore for them. Let not your prayers plead only and altogether for the unconverted, but entreat for our young converts that they may be further edified. It will be an ill day when we are so engaged in seeking lost sheep that we forget the lambs. It would be very mischievous for us to neglect our work at home in order to carry on warfare with the adversary abroad. No, let us cry to God daily in prayer that the stones lately quarried may be built up upon the one foundation, and embedded in the walls of the church of God unto eternal glory. We desire life for the dead, health for the living, and maturity for the healthy. For the deeper instruction of our younger brethren let us pray.

Of this desirable knowledge, what is the measure? We desire for them "that they may be filled with the knowledge of his will." "Filled"—this is grand scholarship, to have the mind, and heart, and the whole of our manhood filled with knowledge. Paul would not have a believer ignorant upon any point: he would have him filled with knowledge, for when a measure is full of wheat there is no room for chaff. True knowledge excludes error. The men that go after false doctrine are usually those who know little of the word of God; being untaught they are unstable, ready to be blown about with every wind of doctrine. If you leave empty spots in your minds unstored with holy teaching, they will be an invitation to the devil to enter in and dwell there. Fill up the soul, and so shut out the enemy. Paul desired the Colossian saints to be filled— filled up to the brim with the knowledge of God's will. Brethren, we would have you know all that you can know of God's truth. Rome flourishes by man's ignorance, but the New Jerusalem rejoices in light. No knowledge of the revealed will of God can ever do you any harm if it be sanctified. Do not be afraid of what they call "high doctrines," or the "deep things of God." They tell us that those things are secrets, and therefore we ought not to pry into them. If they are secrets, there is no fear that anybody can pry into them; but the truths revealed in the word are no longer secrets, seeing that they are revealed to us by the Spirit of God, and as far as they are revealed it should be our desire to understand them, so as to be filled with the knowledge of them.

Let us try to know divine truth more and more intimately. You know a man, for you pass him in the streets with a nod; you know another man far better, for you lodge in the same house with him; you know him best of all when you have shared his trouble, partaken in his joy, and have, in fact, had fellowship with him by blending your two lives in one common stream of friendship. When you learn a spiritual truth endeavour to know it out and out; to know its foundation and upbuilding; to know it by the application of the Spirit to your own soul so that you are filled with it. You may have knowledge in the brain, but it may not run into your spirit, so as to penetrate, and permeate, and saturate your spirit, till you are filled therewith. Oh, to get the gospel into one's entire nature, and to be like the waterpots of Cana, filled up to the brim! Lord, fill thy poor children with the knowledge of thy will!

This makes me notice what the matter of this knowledge is: "filled with the knowledge of his will." What is that? It means the revealed will of God. Paul would have the Colossians know what the Lord has revealed, as far as human mind could grasp it, whether it were doctrine, precept, experience, or prophecy. How well it is to know the preceptive will of God. Our prayer should daily be, "Lord, what wilt thou have me to do?" Lord, teach me what is sin, and what is righteousness, that I may discern things which are excellent. Whereas there are questions in the church of God itself upon what the will of the Lord is, Lord help me not to care to know what is the will of this learned doctor, or what is the will of a certain assembly, but what is the Lord's will. "To the law and to the testimony," this is our touchstone. Our desire is to be filled with the knowledge of the Lord's will so as to do it without fail. Especially would we know the will of God, as it constitutes the gospel; for Jesus says, "This is the will of him that sent me, that every one which seeth the Son, and believeth on him, may have everlasting life." Oh, to know his will in that respect most clearly, so as to go and tell it out on all sides, that men may know the way of life, and may be led into it by our word! Once more we read in 1 Thessalonians 4:3 "This is the will of God, even your sanctification." Oh, to be filled with the knowledge of the Lord's will till you know what sanctification means, and exhibit it in your daily life! It is yours to teach men what God means by holiness. Your mission is not fulfilled, and the will of God is not accomplished unless you are sanctified. This it is with which we need to be filled.

Know anything, know everything that is worth knowing. "That the soul be without knowledge is not good." Never attempt to run side by side with the agnostic whose glory it is that he knows nothing; but let it be your delight to know all that can be learned out of the Book of the Lord, by the teaching of the Holy Ghost. Concentrate your faculties upon the will of God. Here dive into the deeps and climb up to the heights, and be afraid of nothing; ask the Holy Spirit to saturate you with truth, as Gideon's fleece was wet with the dew of heaven, as the golden pot was filled with manna, or as Jordan is filled in the time of harvest, when it overfloweth all its banks.

Still we have not done, for we must now notice the manner as well as the matter of this knowledge: "in all wisdom and spiritual understanding." Wisdom is better than knowledge, for wisdom is knowledge rightly used. Knowledge may find room for folly, but wisdom casts it out. Knowledge may be the horse, but wisdom is the driver. When a man hath knowledge it is like the corn which is laid in the barn; but wisdom is the fine flour prepared for food. We want Christian people not only to know, but to use what they know. Happy is he who knows what to do at the right time! Many people are very knowing half an hour after it is too late; but to be filled with wisdom is to be able at once to apply knowledge rightly in difficult cases. Wisdom enables you to bring your knowledge practically to bear upon life, to separate between the precious and the vile, to deal with your fellow Christians in their different conditions, and to deal with sinners and those that are without. You need wisdom so to conduct your affairs that nothing therein shall scandalize the weak, or bring dishonour upon the name of Christ; for mere knowledge will not suffice for this. Knowledge is the blade, wisdom is the full corn in the ear. Knowledge is the cloth, but wisdom is the garment. Knowledge is the timber, but wisdom hath builded her house. May all our knowledge be sanctified by grace and attended with the guidance of the Spirit that we may become wise to know what the will of the Lord is.

"All wisdom," saith the apostle—many-handed wisdom, wisdom of all sorts, wisdom that will serve you in the shop, wisdom that will be useful in the counting-house, wisdom that will aid the church of God, and wisdom that will guide you if you are cast among the vilest of mankind. May you "be filled with knowledge in all wisdom."

But that wisdom which operates without must be attended by a spiritual understanding which is powerful within. I hardly know how to explain this: it is an inward knowledge of truth, the knowledge of the inward parts of things. It is a spiritual discernment, taste, experience, and reception of truth, whereby the soul feeds upon it, and takes it into herself. We know many men who know much but understand nothing. They accept implicitly what they are taught, but they have never considered it, weighed it, estimated it, found out the roots of it, or seen the heart of it. Oh, to have in the church men full of spiritual understanding! These can say that they have tasted and handled the good word of life, and have proved and tested the truth as it is in Jesus. You know how it was with the sacrifices of old: a man who was poor brought turtle-doves or pigeons, and of these we read of each bird, "The priest shall cleave it with the wings thereof, but shall not divide it asunder:" but a man who was rich in Israel brought a bullock or a sheep, and this offering was not only cleft down the middle, but further divided, and the fat and the "inwards" are mentioned in detail. The poorer sacrifice represents the offering of the uninstructed; they have never rightly divided the word of God, and know not its fulness of meaning; but the man who is rich in grace is comparable to him who brought his bullock; for he can enter into detail and see the secret meanings of the Word. There is a deep which lieth under, and he that is taught of the Lord shall find it. "The secret of the Lord is with them that fear him; and he will show them his covenant;" and blessed are they that are taught of the Lord so as to read the mystery of his grace!

Here, then, is a grand petition for us. To go back to our first head, let our intercessory prayers go up for all our brethren. Lord, teach them thy word. Let them know thy book from cover to cover, and let the truths therein revealed enter into them until they are filled to the brim: then grant thou them the skill to use in daily life the knowledge which thy Spirit has imparted, and may they more and more in their inmost souls be guided into all truth, that they may comprehend with all saints what are the heights, and depths, and. know the love of Christ which passeth knowledge.

III. Now, thirdly, let us see in the text a lesson concerning THE PRACTICAL RESULT OF SPIRITUAL KNOWLEDGE. Paul prays for his friends "that ye might be filled with the knowledge of his will in all wisdom and spiritual understanding; that ye might walk worthy of the Lord unto all pleasing." See, see the drift of his prayer— "that ye may walk." Not that ye might talk, not that ye might sit down and meditate, and enjoy yourselves, but "that ye might walk." He aims at practical results.

He desires that the saints may be instructed so that they may walk according to the best model. By walking worthy of the Lord Jesus we do not understand in any sense that he expected them to possess such worthiness as to deserve to walk with the Lord; but he would have them live in a manner that should be in accordance with their communion with Christ. You would not have a man walk with Christ through the streets to-day clothed in motley garments, or loathsome with filth: would you? No, if a man be a leper, Christ will heal him before he will walk with him. Let not a disciple walk so as to bring disgrace upon his Lord! When you walk with a king, you should be yourself royal in gait; when you commune with a prince you should not act the clown. Dear friends, may you know so much of Jesus that your lives shall become Christ-like, fit to be put side by side with the character of Jesus, worthy of your perfect Lord. This is a high standard, is it not? It is always better to have a high standard than a low one, for you will never go beyond that which you set up as your model. If you get a low standard you will fall below even that. It is an old proverb, "He that aims at the moon will shoot higher than he that aims at a bush." It is well to have no lower standard than the desire to live over again the life of the Lord Jesus—a life of tenderness, a. life of self-sacrifice, a life of generosity, a life of love, a life of honesty, a life of holy service, a life of close communion with God. Mix all virtues in due proportion, and that is the life of Jesus towards which you must press forward with all your heart.

Next, the apostle would have us get knowledge in order that we may so live as to be pleasing to our best friend—

"worthy of the Lord unto all pleasing." Is not that beautiful? To live so as to please God in all respects! Some live to please themselves, and some to please their neighbours, and some to please their wives, and some to please their children, and some live as if they wished to please the devil; but our business is to please him in all things whose servants we are. Without faith it is impossible to please him; so away with unbelief! Without holiness no man shall see him, much less please him; therefore let us follow after holiness, and may the Lord work it in us. "Unto all pleasing"—so that we may please God from the moment we rise in the morning to the time when we lie down, ay, and please him even when we are asleep: that we may eat and drink so as to please him; that we may speak and think so as to please him; that we may go or stay so as to please him; that we may rejoice or suffer so as to please him—"walking worthy of the Lord unto all pleasing." Oh, blessed man, whose life is pleasing to God in all respects! The apostle Paul desires that we may be filled with knowledge to this very end. If I do not know the will of God how can I do the will of God? At least, how can there be anything pleasing to God which is ignorantly done without an intent to do his will? I fear that many children of God grieve their heavenly Father much through sins of ignorance—an ignorance in which they ought not to remain a single day. Be it clearly understood that sins of ignorance are truly sins. They have not about them the venom and the aggravation which are found in sins against light and knowledge, but still they are sins; for the measure of our duty is not our light, but the law of God itself. If a man pleads that he follows his conscience, yet this will not excuse his wrong-doing if his conscience is an unenlightened conscience, and he is content to keep it in the dark. You are to obey the will of the Lord: that will is the standard of the sanctuary. Our conscience is often like a deficient weight, and deceives us; be it ours to gather a clear knowledge of the word, that we may prove what is that perfect and acceptable will of God. The law makes no allowance for errors committed through false weights; when a man says, "I thought my weights and measures were all right," he is not thereby excused. The law deals with facts, not with men's imaginations; the weights must actually be correct, or the penalty is exacted; so is it with conscience, it ought to be instructed in the knowledge of the divine will, and if it is not so, its faultiness affords no justification for evil. Hence the absolute necessity of knowledge in order to true holiness. God grant us grace to know his will, and then to obey it "unto all pleasing."

Look at the text again—"That ye might walk worthy of the Lord unto all pleasing, being fruitful." Paul would have us producing the best fruit. Without knowledge we cannot be fruitful; at least in the points whereof we are ignorant we must fail to bring forth fruit. Therefore would he have us to be right well taught, that we may abundantly produce fruit unto God's glory. He says, "fruitful in every good work"; and this means much. He desires us to be as full of good works as we can hold. Some are hindered in this because they do not know how to set about holy service. How can a man be fruitful as a preacher if he does not know what to preach? True, he may preach the elementary doctrine of the cross, but even that he will be apt to set forth in a blundering manner. For certain, a man cannot teach what he does not know. The zealous, but untaught man, would be much more fruitful if he had a clearer understanding of divine things. In daily life, if in knowledge you are ignorant as to the things of God, you will be ready to become the prey of any false teacher who may chance to pick you up. In hundreds of ways ignorance will make you run risks, lose opportunities of usefulness, and fall into dangerous mistakes. Knowledge is food to the true heart, and strengthens it for the Lord's work. Oh, to have knowledge placed like good soil around the roots of the soul, to fertilize the mind, that thus the clusters of usefulness may be as large as those of Eshcol: beautiful, plentiful, sweet, and full. May our Lord, the King of Israel, to whom the vineyard belongs, receive an abundant reward for all his labour for the vines which he has planted.

There is another note in this verse which I beg you to notice. Paul would have them cultivate a comprehensive variety of the best things. He says—"Fruitful in every good work." Here is room and range enough—"in every good work." Have you the ability to preach the gospel? Preach it! Does a little child need comforting? Comfort it! Can you stand up and vindicate a glorious truth before thousands? Do it! Does a poor saint need a bit of dinner from your table? Send it to her. Let works of obedience, testimony, zeal, charity, piety, and philanthropy all be found in your life. Do not select big things as your special line, but glorify the Lord also in the littles—"fruitful in every good work." You never saw in nature a tree which yielded all sorts of fruit, and you never will. I have seen a tree so grafted that it produced four kinds of fruit at one time, but I remarked that it was a poor business in reference to two of the varieties; for one of the grafts, more natural than the others to the parent stem, drew off the most of the sap, and flourished well, but robbed the other branches. The second sort of fruit managed to live pretty fairly, but not so well as it would have done on its own stem. As for the third and fourth, they were mere attempts at fruit of the smallest size. This tree was shown to me as a great curiosity; it is not likely that practical gardeners will be encouraged by the experiment. But what would you think of a tree upon which you saw grapes, and figs, and olives, and apples, and all other good fruits growing at one time? This is the emblem of what instructed believers will become: they will produce all sorts of goodness and graciousness to the honour of their heavenly Father. I have no doubt that you will naturally abound most in certain good works for which you have the largest capacity, but still nothing ought to come amiss to you. In the great house of the church we want servants who will not be simply cooks or housemaids, but general servants, maids of allwork, prepared to do anything and everything. I have known persons in household employment in England who would not do a turn beyond their special work to save their masters' lives: these are a sort of servants of whom the fewer the better. In India this is carried to a ridiculous extreme. The Hindoo water-bearer will not sweep the house, nor light a fire, nor brush your clothes—he will fetch water, and nothing else: you must, therefore, have a servant for each separate thing, and then each man will do his own little bit, but he will not go an inch beyond. When we enter into Christ's church we should come prepared to wash the saints' feet, or bear their burdens, or bind up their wounds, or fight their foes, or act as steward, or shepherd, or nurse. It has been well said that if two angels in heaven were summoned to serve the Lord, and there were two works to be done, an empire to be ruled, or a crossing to be swept, neither angel would have a choice as to which should be appointed him, but would gladly abide the will of the Lord. Let us be equally prepared for anything, for everything by which fruit can be produced for the Well-beloved.

Why is it that some are not fruitful in this comprehensive way? Because they are not filled with knowledge in all wisdom. When a man says, "You ask me to do the lowest work! Don't you know that I am a man of remarkable ability who should have higher work to do?" I venture to assert that he is an ignorant man. Self-assertion is ignorance on horseback. You have probably read of a certain renowned corporal in the American service a century ago. A general as he rode along saw a body of men endeavouring to lift timber. They were short-handed, and the work lagged, but their famous corporal stood by ordering them about at a magnificent rate. The general passed and said, "Why don't you lend them help and put your shoulder to it?" "Why, sir," said the great little officer, "how can you think of such a thing? Do you know who I am? I am a corporal!" The general got off his horse, pulled off his coat, and helped to move the timber, and by his judicious help the soldiers achieved their task. Then he turned to the high and mighty gentleman and said, "Mr. Corporal, next time you want a man to do such work as this you can send for me: I am General Washington." Just so the Lord Jesus Christ if he were here would gladly do a thousand things which his poor little servants are too great to touch. I know you, dear brother, you are too experienced, too old, too learned to help the Sunday-school! I know you are too respectable to give away a tract! Pray get out of such ignorant ways of thinking, and ask to be useful in all possible ways. If you have done a little, do much; if you have done much, do more; and when you have done more, ask for grace to proceed to the highest possible degree of usefulness for your Lord.

IV. And now, fourthly, notice THE REFLEX ACTION OF HOLINESS UPON KNOWLEDGE. We have only a few moments left; let my few words sink into your hearts. "Fruitful in every good work"—what then? "increasing in the knowledge of God." Look at that. It seems, then, that holiness is the road to knowledge. God has made it so. If any man will do his will he shall know of the doctrine. If you read and study, and cannot make out the meaning of Scripture, get up and do something, and it may be, in the doing of it, you shall discover the secret. Holiness of heart shall increase the illumination of your mind.

Will you kindly observe that this knowledge rises in tone? for Paul first prayed that they "might be filled with the knowledge of God's will"; but now he implores for them an increase in the knowledge of God himself. Oh, blessed growth, first to know the law, and then to know the Law-giver! first to know the precept, and then to know the mouth from which it comes! This is the height of knowledge, to see Christ and know the Father, and learn how to say from the heart, "Truly our fellowship is with the Father, and with his Son Jesus Christ."

I would call your willing attention to another thought. The apostle, if he is to be judged according to his outward language, often utters impossible things, and yet his every sentence is not only full of deep meaning, but is strictly correct. Notice his language here: in the ninth verse he says, "that ye might be filled with the knowledge of his will." Can anything go beyond this? The vessel is filled right up to the brim, what can it have more? Yet the apostle says, "increasing in the knowledge of God." What can that mean? If the mind is full to the brim, how can it receive more? If the man is full of knowledge, how can his knowledge increase? Can there be any increase after that? I propose to you the riddle. Here is the answer of it: Make the vessel larger, and then there can be an increase. This solution of the difficulty requires no great wit to discover it. So that Paul plainly teaches us here that, if we have so increased in knowledge as to be full, he would have us increased in capacity to know yet more; he would have our manhood enlarged, our powers of reception increased, that we might grow from being children to be young men, and from young men to be fathers, and so may be filled— filled, always filled with all the fulness of God! The Lord grant unto us to perceive with humility, that if we are already full of knowledge, we can still advance, for we "have not yet attained." Let no man think that he can go no further. "There is," says Augustine, "a certain perfection according to the measure of this life, and it belongs to that perfection that such a perfect man should know that he is not yet perfect." To that I heartily subscribe. There is a certain fulness to be found in this life according to the measure of a man, and it belongs to that fulness that the man should know that he can yet increase in knowledge. Holy Bernard says "he is not good at all who doth not desire to be better." I also subscribe to that saying. Some might become good if they were not puffed up with the fancy of their own perfection. Others are somewhat commendable, but will never grow because they judge themselves to be full-grown already. I would have you filled, and yet have room for more: filled with all knowledge, filled with all holiness, filled with the indwelling Spirit, filled with God, and yet increasing in knowledge, in holiness, in likeness to God, and in all good things evermore to his glory. The Lord add his blessing for Jesus' sake. Amen.

4

SPECIAL THANKSGIVING TO THE FATHER (1860)

"Giving thanks unto the Father, which hath made us meet to be partakers of the inheritance of the saints in light: who hath delivered us from the power of darkness, and hath translated us into the kingdom of his dear Son."—Col 1:12, 13.

"True indeed the older we grow the more grace we have tasted, the riper we are becoming, and the fitter to be housed in heaven."

—

THIS passage is a mine of riches. I can anticipate the difficulty in preaching and the regret in concluding we shall experience this evening because we are not able to dig out all the gold which lies in this precious vein. We lack the power to grasp and the time to expatiate upon that volume of truths which is here condensed into a few short sentences.

We are exhorted to "give thanks unto the Father." This counsel is at once needful and salutary. I think, my brethren, we scarcely need to be told to give thanks unto the Son. The remembrance of that bleeding body hanging upon the cross is ever present to our faith. The nails and the spear, his griefs, the anguish of his soul, and his sweat of agony, make such tender touching appeals to our gratitude—these will prevent us always from ceasing our songs, and sometimes fire our hearts with rekindling rapture in praise of the man Christ Jesus. Yes, we will bless thee, dearest Lord; our souls are all on fire. As we survey the wondrous cross, we cannot but shout—

> "O for this love let rocks and hills
>   Their lasting silence break,
> And all harmonious human tongues
>   The Saviour's praises speak."

It is in a degree very much the same with the Holy Spirit. I think we are compelled to feel every day our dependence upon his constant influence. He abides with us as a present and personal Comforter and Counsellor. We, therefore, do praise the Spirit of Grace, who hath made our heart his temple, and who works in us all that is gracious, virtuous, and well-pleasing in the sight of God. If there be any one Person in the Trinity whom we are more apt to forget than another in our praises, it is God the Father. In fact there are some who even get a wrong idea of Him, a slanderous idea of that God whose name is LOVE. They imagine that love dwelt in Christ, rather than in the Father; and that our salvation is rather due to the Son and the Holy Spirit, than to our Father God. Let us not be of the number of the ignorant, but let us receive this truth. We are as much indebted to the Father as to any other Person of the Sacred Three. He as much and as truly loves us as any of the adorable Three Persons. He is as truly worthy of our highest praise as either the Son or the Holy Spirit.

A remarkable fact, which we should always bear in mind, is this:—in the Holy Scriptures most of the operations which are set down as being the works of the Spirit, are in other Scriptures ascribed to God the Father. Do we say it is God the Spirit that quickens the sinner who is dead in sin? it is true; but you will find in another passage it is said, "The Father quickeneth whom he will." Do we say that the Spirit is the sanctifier, and that the sanctification of the soul is wrought by the Holy Ghost? You will find a passage in the opening of the Epistle of St. Jude, in which it is said, "Sanctified by God the Father." Now, how are we to account for this? I think it may be explained thus. God the Spirit cometh from God the Father, and therefore whatever acts are performed by the Spirit are truly done by the Father, because he sendeth forth the Spirit. And again, the Spirit is often the instrument—though I say not this in any way to derogate from his glory—he is often the instrument with which the Father works. It is the Father who says to the dry bones, live; it is the Spirit who, going forth with the divine word, makes them live. The quickening is due as much to the word as to the influence that went with the word; and as the word came with all the bounty of free grace and goodwill from the Father, the quickening is due to him. It is true that the seal on our hearts is the Holy Spirit; he is the seal, but it is the Eternal Father's hand that stamps the seal; the Father communicates the Spirit to seal our adoption. The works of the Spirit are, many of them, I repeat it again, attributed to the Father, because he worketh in, through, and by the Spirit.

The works of the Son of God, I ought to observe are every one of them in intimate connection with the Father. If the Son comes into the world, it is because the Father sends him; if the Son calls his people, it is because his Father gave this people into his hands. If the Son redeems the chosen race, is not the Son himself the Father's gift, and doth not God send his Son into the world that we may live through him? So that the Father, the great Ancient of Days, is ever to be extolled; and we must never omit the full homage of our hearts to him when we sing that sacred doxology,

"Praise Father, Son, and Holy Ghost."

In order to excite your gratitude to God the Father to-night, I propose to dilate a little upon this passage, as God the Holy Spirit shall enable me. If you will look at the text, you will see two blessings in it. The first has regard to the future; it is a meetness for the inheritance of the saints in light. The second blessing, which must go with the first, for indeed it is the cause of the first, the effective cause, has relation to the past. Here we read of our deliverance from the power of darkness. Let us meditate a little upon each of these blessings, and then, in the third place, I will endeavour to show the relation which exists between the two.

I. The first blessing introduced to our notice is this—"God the Father has made us meet to be partakers of the inheritance of the saints in light." It is a PRESENT BLESSING. Not a mercy laid up for us in the covenant, which we have not yet received, but it is a blessing which every true believer already has in his hand. Those mercies in the covenant of which we have the earnest now while we wait for the full possession, are just as rich, and just as certain as those which have been already with abundant lovingkindness bestowed on us; but still they are not so precious in our enjoyment. The mercy we have in store, and in hand, is after all, the main source of our present comfort. And oh what a blessing this! "Made meet for the inheritance of the saints in light." The true believer is fit for heaven; he is meet to be a partaker of the inheritance— and that now, at this very moment. What does this mean? Does it mean that the believer is perfect; that he is free from sin? No, my brethren, where shall you ever find such perfection in this world? If no man can be a believer but the perfect man, then what has the perfect man to believe? Could he not walk by sight? When he is perfect, he may cease to be a believer. No, brethren, it is not such perfection that is meant, although perfection is implied, and assuredly will be given as the result. Far less does this mean that we have a right to eternal life from any doings of our own. We have a fitness for eternal life, a meetness for it, but we have no desert of it. We deserve nothing of God even now, in ourselves, but his eternal wrath and his infinite displeasure. What, then, does it mean? Why, it means just this: we are so far meet that we are accepted in the Beloved, adopted into the family, and fitted by divine approbation to dwell with the saints in light. There is a woman chosen to be a bride; she is fitted to be married, fitted to enter into the honourable state and condition of matrimony; but at present she has not on the bridal garment, she is not like the bride adorned for her husband. You do not see her yet robed in her elegant attire, with her ornaments upon her, but you know she is fitted to be a bride, she is received and welcomed as such in the family of her destination. So Christ has chosen his Church to be married to him; she has not yet put on her bridal garment, and all that beautiful array in which she shall stand before the Father's throne, but notwithstanding, there is such a fitness in her to be the bride of Christ, when she shall have bathed herself for a little while, and lain for a little while in the bed of spices—there is such a fitness in her character, such a grace-given adaptation in her to become the royal bride of her glorious Lord, and to become a partaker of the enjoyments of bliss—that it may be said of the church as a whole, and ot every member of it, that they are "meet for the inheritance of the saints in light."

The Greek word, moreover, bears some such meaning as this, though I cannot give the exact idiom, it is always difficult when a word is not used often. This word is only used twice, that I am aware of, in the New Testament. The word may be employed for "suitable," or, I think, "sufficient." "He hath made us meet"—sufficient—"to be partakers of the inheritance of the saints in light." But I cannot give my idea without borrowing another figure. When a child is born, it is at once endowed with all the faculties of humanity. If those powers are awanting at first, they will not come afterwards. It has eyes, it has hands, it has feet, and all its physical organs. These of course are as it were in embryo. The senses though perfect at first, must be gradually developed, and the understanding gradually matured. It can see but little, it cannot discern distances; it can hear, but it cannot hear distinctly enough at first to know from what direction the sound comes; but you never find a new leg, a new arm, a new eye, or a new ear growing on that child. Each of these powers will expand and enlarge, but still there is the whole man there at first, and the child is sufficient for a man. Let but God in his infinite providence cause it to feed, and give it strength and increase, it has sufficient for manhood. It does not want either arm or leg, nose or ear; you cannot make it grow a new member; nor does it require a new member either; all are there. In like manner, the moment a man is regenerated, there is every faculty in his new creation that there shall be, even when he gets to heaven. It only needs to be developed and brought out: he will not have a new power, he will not have a new grace, he will have those which he had before, developed and brought out. Just as we are told by the careful observer, that in the acorn there is in embryo every root and every bough and every leaf of the future tree, which only requires to be developed and brought out in their fulness. So, in the true believer, there is a sufficiency or meetness for the inheritance of the saints in light. All that he requires is, not that a new thing should be implanted, but that that which God has put there in the moment of regeneration, shall be cherished and nurtured, and made to grow and increase, till it comes unto perfection and he enters into "the inheritance of the saints in light." This is, as near as I can give it to you, the exact meaning and literal interpretation of the text, as I understand it.

But you may say to me, "In what sense is this meetness or fitness for eternal life the work of God the Father? Are we already made meet for heaven? How is this the Father's work?" Look at the text a moment, and I will answer you in three ways.

What is heaven? We read it is an inheritance. Who are fit for an inheritance? Sons. Who makes us sons? "Behold what manner of love the Father hath bestowed upon us, that we should be called the sons of God." A son is fitted for an inheritance. The moment the son is born he is fitted to be an heir. All that is wanted is that he shall grow up and be capable of possession. But he is fit for an inheritance at first. If he were not a son he could not inherit as an heir. Now, as soon as ever we become sons we are meet to inherit. There is in us an adaptation, a power and possibility for us to have an inheritance. This is the prerogative of the Father, to adopt us into his family, and to "beget us again unto a lively hope by the resurrection of Jesus Christ from the dead." And do you not see, that as adoption is really the meetness for inheritance, it is the Father who hath "made us meet to be partakers of the inheritance of the saints in light?"

Again, heaven is an inheritance; but whose inheritance is it? It is an inheritance of the saints. It is not an inheritance of sinners, but of saints—that is, of the holy ones—of those who have been made saints by being sanctified. Turn then, to the Epistle of Jude, and you will see at once who it is that sanctifies. You will observe the moment you fix your eye upon the passage that it is God the Father. In the first verse you read, "Jude, the servant of Jesus Christ, and brother of James, to them that are sanctified by God the Father." It is an inheritance for saints: and who are saints? The moment a man believes in Christ, he may know himself to have been truly set apart in the covenant decree; and he finds that consecration, if I may so speak, verified in his own experience, for he has now become "a new creature in Christ Jesus," separated from the rest of the world, and then it is manifest and made known that God has taken him to be his son for ever. The meetness which I must have, in order to enjoy the inheritance of the saints in light, is my becoming a son. God hath made me and all believers sons, therefore we are meet for the inheritance; so then that meetness has come from the Father. How meetly therefore doth the Father claim our gratitude, our adoration and our love!

You will however observe, it is not merely said that heaven is the inheritance of the saints, but that it is "the inheritance of the saints in light." So the saints dwell in light—the light of knowledge, the light of purity, the light of joy, the light of love, pure ineffable love, the light of everything that is glorious and ennobling. There they dwell, and if I am to appear meet for that inheritance, what evidence must I have? I must have light shining into my own soul. But where can I get it? Do I not read that "every good gift and every perfect gift is from above, and cometh down"—yea verily, but from whom? From the Spirit? No—"from the Father of lights, with whom is no variableness, neither shadow of turning." The preparation to enter into the inheritance in light is light; and light comes from the Father of lights; therefore, my meetness, if I have light in myself, is the work of the Father, and I must give him praise. Do you see then, that as there are three words used here—"the inheritance of the saints in light," so we have a threefold meetness? We are adopted and made sons. God hath sanctified us and set us apart. And then, again, he hath put light into our hearts. All this, I say, is the work of the Father, and in this sense, we are "meet to be partakers of the inheritance of the saints in light."

A few general observations here. Brethren, I am persuaded that if an angel from heaven were to come to-night and single out any one believer from the crowd here assembled, there is not one believer that is unfit to be taken to heaven. You may not be ready to be taken to heaven now; that is to say, if I foresaw that you were going to live, I would tell you you were unfit to die, in a certain sense. But were you to die now in your pew, if you believe in Christ, you are fit for heaven. You have a meetness even now which would take you there at once, without being committed to purgatory for a season. You are even now fit to be "partakers of the inheritance of the saints in light." You have but to gasp out your last breath and you shall be in heaven, and there shall not be one spirit in heaven more fit for heaven than you, nor one soul more adapted for the place than you are. You shall be just as fitted for its element as those who are nearest to the eternal throne.

Ah! this makes the heirs of glory think much of God the Father. When we reflect, my brethren, upon our state by nature, and how fit we are to be fire-brands in the flames of hell—yet to think that we are this night, at this very moment if Jehovah willed it, fit to sweep the golden harps with joyful fingers, that this head is fit this very night to

wear the everlasting crown, that these loins are fit to be
girded with that fair white robe throughout eternity, I say,
this makes us think gratefully of God the Father; this
makes us clap our hands with joy, and say, "Thanks be
unto God the Father, who hath made us meet to be
partakers of the inheritance of the saints in light." Do ye
not remember the penitent thief? It was but a few minutes
before that he had been cursing Christ. I doubt not that he
had joined with the other, for it is said, "They that were
crucified with him reviled him." Not one, but both; they
did it. And then a gleam of supernatural glory lit up the
face of Christ, and the thief saw and believed. And Jesus
said unto him, "Verily I say unto thee, this day," though
the sun is setting, "this day shalt thou be with me in
Paradise." No long preparation required, no sweltering in
purifying fires. And so shall it be with us. We may have
been in Christ Jesus to our own knowledge but three
weeks, or we may have been in him for ten years, or
threescore years and ten—the date of our conversion
makes no difference in our meetness for heaven, in a
certain sense. True indeed the older we grow the more
grace we have tasted, the riper we are becoming, and the
fitter to be housed in heaven; but that is in another sense
of the word,—the Spirit's meetness which he gives. But
with regard to that meetness which the Father gives, I
repeat, the blade of corn, the blade of gracious wheat that
has just appeared above the surface of conviction, is as fit
to be carried up to heaven as the full-grown corn in the
ear. The sanctification wherewith we are sanctified by God
the Father is not progressive, it is complete at once; we are
now adapted for heaven, now fitted for it, and we shall be

by-and-bye completely ready for it, and shall enter into the joy of our Lord.

Into this subject I might have entered more fully; but I have not time. I am sure I have left some knots untied, and you must untie them if you can yourselves; and let me recommend you to untie them on your knees—the mysteries of the kingdom of God are studied much the best when you are in prayer.

II. The second mercy is A MERCY THAT LOOKS BACK. We sometimes prefer the mercies that look forward, because they unfold such a bright prospect.

"Sweet fields beyond the swelling flood."

But here is a mercy that looks backward; turns its back, as it were, on the heaven of our anticipation, and looks back on the gloomy past, and the dangers from which we have escaped. Let us read the account of it—"Who hath delivered us from the power of darkness, and hath translated us into the kingdom of his dear Son." This verse is an explanation of the preceding, as we shall have to show in a few minutes. But just now let us survey this mercy by itself. Ah! my brethren, what a description have we here of what maner of men we used to be. We were under "the power of darkness." Since I have been musing on this text, I have turned these words over and over in my mind—"the power of darkness!" It seems to me one of the most awful expressions that man ever attempted to expound. I think I could deliver a discourse from it, if God the Spirit helped me, which might make every bone in your body shake. "The power of darkness!" We all know that there is a moral darkness which exercises its awful spell over the mind of the sinner. Where God is unacknowledged the mind is void of judgment. Where God is unworshipped the heart of man becomes a ruin. The chambers of that dilapidated herrt are haunted by ghostly fears and degraded superstitions. The dark places of that reprobate mind are tenanted by vile lusts and noxious passions, like vermin and reptiles, from which in open daylight we turn with disgust. And even natural darkness is tremendous. In the solitary confinement which is practised in some of our penitentiaries the very worst results would be produced if the treatment were prolonged. If one of you were to be taken to-night and led into some dark cavern, and left there, I can imagine that for a moment, not knowing your fate, you might feel a child-like kind of interest about it;—there might be, perhaps, a laugh as you found yourselves in the dark; there might for the moment, from the novelty of the position, be some kind of curiosity excited. There might, perhaps, be a flush of silly joy. In a little time you might endeavour to compose yourself to sleep; possibly you might sleep; but if you should awake, and still find yourself down deep in the bowels of earth, where never a ray of sun or candle light could reach you; do you know the next feeling that would come over you? It would be a kind of idiotic thoughtlessness. You would find it impossible to control your desperate imagination. You heart would say, "O God I am alone, alone, alone, in this dark place." How would you cast your eyeballs all around, and never catching a gleam of light, your mind would begin to fail. Your next stage would be one of increasing terror. You would fancy that you saw something, and then you would cry, "Ah! I would I could see something, were it foe or fiend!" You would feel the dark sides of your dungeon. You would begin to "scribble on the walls," like David before king Achish. Agitation would cease hold upon you, and if you were kept there much longer, delirium and death would be the consequence. We have heard of many who have been taken from the penitentiary to the lunatic asylum; and the lunacy is produced partly by the solitary confinement, and partly by the darkness in which they are placed. In a report lately written by the Chaplain of Newgate, there are some striking reflections upon the influence of darkness in a way of discipline. Its first effect is to shut the culprit up to his own reflections, and make him realize his true position in the iron grasp of the outraged law. Methinks the man that has defied his keepers, and come in there cursing and swearing, when he has found himself alone in darkness, where he cannot even hear the rattling of carriages along the streets, and can see no light whatever, is presently cowed; he gives in, he grows tame. "The power of darkness" literally is something awful. If I had time, I would enlarge upon this subject. We cannot properly describe what "the power of darkness" is, even in this world. The sinner is plunged into the darkness of his sins, and he sees nothing, he knows nothing. Let him remain there a little longer, and that joy of curiosity, that hectic joy which he now has in the path of sin, will die away, and there will come over him a spirit of slumber. Sin will make him drowsy, so that he will not hear the voice of the ministry, crying to him to escape for his life. Let him continue in it, and it will by-and-bye make him spiritually an idiot. He will become so set in sin, that common reason will be lost on him. All the arguments that a sensible man will receive, will be only wasted on him. Let him go on, and he will proceed from bad to worse, till he acquires the raving mania of a desperado in sin; and let death step in, and the darkness will have produced its full effect; he will come into the delirious madness of hell. Ah! it needs but the power of sin to make a man more truly hideous than human thought can realize, or language paint. Oh "the power of darkness!"

Now, my brethren, all of us were under this power once. It is but a few months—a few weeks with some of you— since you were under the power of darkness and of sin. Some of you had only got as far as the curiosity of it; others had got as far as the sleepiness of it; a good many of you had got as far as the apathy of it; and I do not know but some of you had got almost to the terror of it. You had so cursed and swore; so yelled ye out your blasphemies, that you seemed to be ripening for hell; but, praised and blessed be the name of the Father, he has "translated you from the power of darkness, into the kingdom of his dear Son."

Having thus explained this term, "the power of darkness," to show you what you were, let us take the next word, "and hath translated us." What a singular word this— "translated"—is. I dare say you think it means the process by which a word is interpreted, when the sense is retained, while the expression is rendered in another language. That is one meaning of the word "translation," but it is not the meaning here. The word is used by Josephus in this sense—the taking away of a people who have been dwelling in a certain country, and planting them in another place. This is called a translation. We sometimes hear of a bishop being translated or removed from one see to another. Now, if you want to have the idea explained, give me your attention while I bring out an amazing instance of a great translation. The children of Israel were in Egypt under taskmasters that oppressed them very sorely, and brought them into iron bondage. What did God do for these people? There were two millions of them. He did not temper the tyranny of the tyrant; he did not influence his mind, to give them a little more liberty; but he translated his people; he took the whole two millions bodily, with a high hand and outstretched arm, and led them through the wilderness, and translated them into the kingdom of Canaan; and there they were settled. What an achievement was that, when, with their flocks and their herds, and their little ones, the whole host of Israel went out of Egypt, crossed the Jordan, and came into Canaan! My dear brethren, the whole of it was not equal to the achievement of God's powerful grace, when he brings one poor sinner out of the region of sin into the kingdom of holiness and peace. It was easier for God to bring Israel out of Egypt, to split the Red Sea, to make a highway through the pathless wilderness, to drop manna from heaven, to send the whirlwind to drive out the Kings; it was easier for Omnipotence to do all this, than to translate a man from the power of darkness into the kingdom of his dear Son. This is the grandest achievement of Omnipotence. The sustenance of the whole universe, I do believe, is even less than this—the changing of a bad heart, the subduing of an iron will. But thanks be unto the Father, he has done all that for you and for me. He has brought us out of darkness; he has translated us, taken up the old tree that has struck its roots never so deep—taken it up, blessed be God, roots and all, and planted it in a goodly soil. He had to cut the top off, it is true—the high branches of our pride; but the tree has grown better in the new soil than it ever did before. Who ever heard of moving so huge a plant as a man who has grown fifty years old in sin? Oh! what wonders hath our Father done for us! He has taken the wild leopard of the wood, tamed it into a lamb, and purged away its spots He has regenerated the poor Ethiop—oh, how black we were by nature—our blackness was more than skin deep; it went to the centre of our hearts; but, blessed be his name, he hath washed us white, and is still carrying on the divine operation, and he will yet completely deliver us from every taint of sin, and will finally bring us into the kingdom of his dear Son. Here, then, in the second mercy, we discern from what we were delivered, and how we were delivered—God the Father hath "translated" us.

But where are we now? Into what place is the believer brought, when he is brought out of the power of darkness? He is brought into the kingdom of God's dear Son. Into what other kingdom would the Christian desire to be brought? Brethren, a republic may sound very well in theory, but in spiritual matters, the last thing we want is a republic. We want a kingdom. I love to have Christ an absolute monarch in the heart. I do not want to have a doubt about it. I want to give up all my liberty to him, for I feel that I never shall be free till my self-control is all gone; that I shall never have my will truly free till it is bound in the golden fetters of his sweet love. We are brought into a kingdom—he is Lord and Sovereign, and he has made us "kings and priests unto our God," and we shall reign with him. The proof that we are in this kingdom must consist in our obedience to our King. Here, perhaps, we may raise many causes and questions, but surely we can say after all, though we have offended our King many times, yet our heart is loyal to him. "Oh, thou precious Jesus! we would obey thee, and yield submission to every one of thy laws; our sins are not wilful and beloved sins, but though we fall we can truly say, that we would be holy as thou art holy, our heart is true towards thy statutes; Lord, help us to run in the way of thy commandments."

So, you see, this mercy which God the Father hath given to us, this second of these present mercies, is, that he hath "translated us out of the power of darkness into the kingdom of his dear Son." This is the Father's work. Shall we not love God the Father from this day forth? Will we not give him thanks, and sing our hymns to him, and exalt and triumph in his great name?

III. Upon the third point, I shall be as brief as possible; it is to SHOW THE CONNECTION BETWEEN THE TWO VERSES.

When I get a passage of Scripture to meditate upon, I like, if I can, to see its drift; then I like to examine its various parts, and see if I can understand each separate clause; and then I want to go back again, and see what one clause has to do with another. I looked and looked again at this text, and wondered what connection there could be between the two verses. "Giving thanks unto God the Father, who hath made us meet to be partakers of the inheritance of the saints in light." Well, that is right enough; we can see how this is the work of God the Father, to make us meet to go to heaven. But has the next verse, the 13th, anything to do with our meetness?—"Who hath delivered us from the power of darkness, and hath translated us into the kingdom of his dear Son." Well, I looked it over, and I said I will read it in this way. I see the 12th verse tells me that the inheritance of heaven is the inheritance of light. Is heaven light? Then I can see my meetness for it as described in the 13th verse.—He hath delivered me from the power of darkness. Is not that the same thing? If I am delivered from the power of darkness, is not that being made meet to dwell in light? If I am now brought out of darkness into light, and am walking in the light, is not that the very meetness which is spoken of in the verse before? Then I read again. It says they are saints. Well, the saints are a people that obey the Son. Here is my meetness then in the 13th verse, where it says "He hath translated me from the power of darkness into the kingdom of his dear Son." So that I not only have the light, but the sonship too, for I am in "the kingdom of his dear Son." But how about the inheritance? Is there anything about that in the 13th verse? It is an inheritance; shall I find anything about a meetness for it there? Yes, I find that I am in the kingdom of his dear Son. How came Christ to have a kingdom? Why, by inheritance. Then it seems I am in his inheritance; and if I am in his inheritance here, then I am meet to be in it above, for I am in it already. I am even now part of it and partner of it, since I am in the kingdom which he inherits from his Father, and therefore there is the meetness.

I do not know whether I have put this plainly enough before you. If you will be kind enough to look at your Bible, I will just recapitulate. You see, heaven is a place of light; when we are brought out of darkness, that, of course, is the meetness for light. It is a place for sons; when we are brought into the kingdom of God's dear Son, we are of course made sons; so that there is the meetness for it. It is an inheritance; and when we are brought into the inherited kingdom of God's dear Son, we enjoy the inheritance now, and consequently are fitted to enjoy it for ever.

Having thus shown the connection between these verses, I propose now to close with a few general observations. I like so to expound the Scripture, that we can draw some practical inferences from it. Of course the first inference is this: let us from this night forward never omit God the Father in our praises. I think I have said this already six times over in the sermon. Why I am repeating it so often, is that we may never forget it. Martin Luther said he preached upon justification by faith every day in the week, and then the people would not understand. There are some truths, I believe, that need to be said over and over again, either because our silly hearts will not receive, or our treacherous memories will not hold them. Sing, I beseech you, habitually, the praises of the Father in heaven, as you do the praises of the Son hanging upon the cross. Love as truly God, the ever-living God, as you love Jesus the God-man, the Saviour who once died for you. That is the great inference.

Yet another inference arises. Brothers and sisters, are you conscious to-night that you are not now what you once were? Are you sure that the power of darkness does not now rest upon you, that you love divine knowledge, that you are panting after heavenly joys? Are you sure that you have been "translated into the kingdom of God's dear Son?" Then never be troubled about thoughts of death, because, come death whenever it may, you are meet to be a "partaker of the inheritance of the saints in light." Let no thought distress you about death's coming to you at an unseasonable hour. Should it come to-morrow, should it come now, if your faith is fixed on nothing less than Jesu's blood and righteousness, you shall see the face of God with acceptance. I have that consciousness in my soul, by the witness of the Holy Spirit, of my adoption into the family of God, that I feel that though I should never preach again, but should lay down my body and my charge together, ere I should reach my home, and rest in my bed, "I know that my Redeemer liveth," and more, that I should be a "partaker of the inheritance of the saints in light." It is not always that one feels that; but I would have you never rest satisfied till you do, till you know your meetness, till you are conscious of it; until, moreover, you are panting to be gone, because you feel that you have powers which never can be satisfied short of heaven—powers which heaven only can employ.

One more reflection lingers behind. There are some of you here that cannot be thought by the utmost charity of judgment, to be "meet for the inheritance of the saints in light." Ah! if a wicked man should go to heaven without being converted, heaven would be no heaven to him. Heaven is not adapted for sinners; it is not a place for them. If you were to take a Hottentot who has long dwelt at the equator up to where the Esquimaux are dwelling, and tell him that you would show him the aurora, and all the glories of the North Pole, the poor wretch could not appreciate them; he would say, "It is not the element for me; it is not the place where I could rest happy! And if you were to take, on the other hand, some dwarfish dweller in the north, down to the region where trees grow to a stupendous height, and where the spices give their balmy odours to the gale, and bid him live there under the torrid zone, he could enjoy nothing; he would say, "This is not the place for me, because it is not adapted to my nature." Or if you were to take the vulture, that has never fed on anything but carrion, and put it into the noblest dwelling you could make for it, and feed it with the daintiest meals, it would not be happy because it is not food that is adapted for it. And you, sinner, you are nothing but a carrion vulture; nothing makes you happy but sin; you do not want too much psalm singing, do you? Sunday is a dull day to you; you like to get it over, you do not care about your Bible; you would as soon there should be no Bible at all. You find that going to a meeting-house or a church is very dull work indeed. Oh then you will not be troubled with that in eternity; do not agitate yourself. If you love not God, and die as you are, you shall go to your own company, you shall go to your jolly mates, you shall go to your good fellows; those who have been your mates on earth shall be your mates for ever; but you shall go to the Prince of those good fellows, unless you repent and be converted. Where God is you cannot come. It is not an element suited to you. As well place a bird at the bottom of the sea, or a fish in the air, as place an ungodly sinner in heaven. What is to be done then? You must have a new nature. I pray God to give it to you. Remember if now you feel your need of a Saviour, that is the beginning of the new nature. "Believe on the Lord Jesus Christ;" cast yourselves simply on him, trust in nothing but his blood, and then the new nature shall be expanded, and you shall be made meet by the Holy Spirit's operations to be a "partaker of the inheritance of the saints in light." There is many a man who has come into this house of prayer, many a man is now present, who has come in here a rollicking fellow, fearing neither God nor devil. Many a man has come from the ale house up to this place. If he had died then, where would his soul have been? But the Lord that very night met him. There are trophies of that grace present here to-night. You can say, "Thanks be to the Father, who hath brought us out of the power of darkness, and translated us into the kingdom of his dear Son." And if God has done that for some, why cannot he do it for others? Why need you despair, O poor sinner? If thou art here to-night, the worst sinner out of hell, remember, the gate of mercy stands wide open, and Jesus bids thee come. Conscious of thy guilt, flee, flee to him. Look to his cross. and thou shalt find pardon in his veins, and life in his death.

5
A ROUND OF DELIGHTS (1877)

"Now the God of hope fill you with all joy and peace in believing, that ye may abound in hope, through the power of the Holy Ghost."—Romans 15:13.

"Every promise is meant to inspire the believer with hope; therefore use it to that end. Use the written word as the source of comfort, and do not look for dreams, excitements, impressions, or feelings. Faith deals with the Scriptures and with the God of hope as therein revealed, and out of these it draws its fulness of joy and peace."

———

THIS is one of the richest passages in the Word of God. It is so full of instruction that I cannot hope to bring out even so much as a tithe of its teaching. The apostle desired for the Roman Christians that they might be in the most delightful state of mind, that they should be filled with joy and peace, and that this should lead on to yet further expectations, and create an abundance of hope in their souls. See, dear friends, the value of prayer, for if Paul longs to see his friends attain the highest possible condition, he prays for them. What will not prayer do? Whatsoever thou desirest for thyself, or for another, let thy desire be prepared like sweet spices and compounded into a supplication, and present it unto God, and the benediction will come.

I gather, also, from Paul's making this state of happiness a subject of request unto God, that it is possible for it to be attained. We may be filled with joy and peace in believing, and may abound in hope. There is no reason why we should hang our heads and live in perpetual doubt. We may not only be somewhat comforted, but we may be full of joy; we may not only have occasional quiet, but we may dwell in peace, and delight ourselves in the abundance of it. These great privileges are attainable, or the apostle would not have made them the subjects of prayer. Ay, and they are possible for us, as the meaning of the Epistle to the Romans was not exhausted upon the Romans, so this text belongeth to us also; and the words before us still rise to heaven as the prayer of the apostle for us, upon whom the ends of the earth are come, that we also may be filled with joy and peace, and abound in hope through the Holy Ghost. The sweetest delights are still grown in Zion's gardens, and are to be enjoyed by us; and shall they be within our reach and not be grasped? Shall a life of joy and peace be attainable, and shall we miss it through unbelief? God forbid. Let us, as believers, resolve that whatsoever of privilege is to be enjoyed we will enjoy it; whatsoever of lofty experience is to be realized, we will, by God's gracious help, ascend to it: for we wish to know to the full the things which are freely given to us of God.

Not, however, in our own strength will we thus resolve, for this condition of faith, and joy, and peace must be wrought in us by God alone. This is clear enough in the text, for it is the God of hope who alone can fill us with joy and peace; and yet again, our hope which is to abound will only abound through the power of the Holy Ghost. The fact that the happy condition described is sought by prayer is a plain evidence that the blessing comes from a divine source, and the prayer itself is so worded that the doctrine is prominently presented to the mind. So, brethren, while we resolve to obtain everything of privilege that is obtainable, let us set about our effort in divine power, not depending upon our resolutions, but looking for the power of the Holy Ghost and the energy of the God of hope.

I shall want you to follow me whilst I notice concerning the blessed state of fulness of joy and peace, first, whence it comes; secondly, what it is, taking its delights in detail; and then, thirdly, what it leads to. We are to be filled with joy and peace, that "we may abound in hope through the power of the Holy Ghost."

I. If there be, then, such a condition as being divinely filled with all joy and peace in believing, WHENCE DOES IT COME? The answer is, it comes from "the God of hope." But in order that we may see how it comes let us look a little at the chapter in which we find our text, for the connection is instructive.

To know joy and peace through believing we must begin by knowing what is to be believed, and this we must learn from holy Scripture, for there he is revealed as the God of hope. Unless God had revealed himself, we could not have guessed at hope, but the Scriptures of truth are windows of hope to us. Will you kindly read the fourth verse of the chapter and note how strikingly parallel it is to our text— "For whatsoever things were written aforetime were written for our learning, that we through patience and comfort of the Scriptures might have hope." See, then, the God of hope is revealed in Scripture with the design of inspiring us with hope. If we would be filled with faith, joy, and peace, it must be by believing the truths set forth in the Scriptures. Before we have any inward ground of hope, God himself, as revealed in the Bible, must be our hope. We must not ask for joy first and then found our faith upon it, but our joy must grow out of our faith, and that must rest upon God alone. Our apostle sets us an example of how to use the Scriptures, for in this chapter he searches out the truth from Moses, and David, and Isaiah, and then places one text with another and gets a clear view of the testimony of God. What is very much to our point, he sees in those Scriptures that to us Gentiles God has of old been set forth in the Scriptures as the God of hope. Aforetime it seemed as if salvation were of the Jews and of the Jews alone, and we were shut out; but now, on turning to the Old Testament itself, we discover that God had spoken good things concerning us before we knew him. There was always hope for the Gentiles, and though Israel perceived it not, yet patriarchs and kings and prophets full often spake words which could not otherwise be interpreted. "In thee and in thy seed shall all the nations of the earth be blessed" is a promise which overleaped the bounds of Canaan. As, then, by searching the apostle found in the word of God hope for the Gentiles, so will the most heavy laden and burdened spirit discover sources of consolation if the Bible be diligently read and faithfully believed. Every promise is meant to inspire the believer with hope; therefore use it to that end. Use the written word as the source of comfort, and do not look for dreams, excitements, impressions, or feelings. Faith deals with the Scriptures and with the God of hope as therein revealed, and out of these it draws its fulness of joy and peace. Beloved, if you desire to get faith in Christ, or to increase it, be diligent in knowing and understanding the gospel of your salvation as set forth in the word of God. "Faith cometh by hearing," or by reading the word of God. How shall you believe that which you do not know? Do not at once make an effort to believe before you are instructed, but first know what God hath revealed, see how he hath displayed to you the hope of everlasting life, and then believe with all your heart the testimony of God. Every promise and word of God must be to you a foundation most sure and steadfast whereon to build your hope. Let your anchor grasp and hold to each revealed truth, whatever your feelings may be. We begin then by saying that fulness of joy and peace comes to us from the God of hope as he reveals himself in holy writ. As it is written, "Hear, and your soul shall live," so do we find that we must hear if our soul is to rejoice.

Now, it so happens that the Scriptures were not only written that the Gentiles might have hope, but that they might have joy. I ask you to notice the passages quoted by the apostle, for at least the last three of them call us to joy. Thus in verse 10, Moses saith, "Rejoice, ye Gentiles, with his people." If there be any joy for the elect nation, it is for us also who believe. If there be any joy for Israel redeemed out of Egypt, led through the Red Sea, fed with manna, and brought to the borders of Canaan, that joy is for us also; if any joy over the burnt offering, if any joy at the paschal supper, if any delight at the jubilee, all that joy may be shared by us, for thus saith the Lord, "Rejoice, ye Gentiles, with his people." Joy in their joy. Again, David saith (verse 11), "Praise the Lord, all ye Gentiles; and laud him, all ye people." Now, where there is praise there is joy, for joy is a component element of it. They that praise the Lord aright rejoice before him. Go, ye Gentiles, when David bids you thus unite with Israel in praising God, he bids you take full possession of the joy which moves the favoured nation to magnify the Lord. Again, Isaiah says, "There shall be a root of Jesse, and he that shall rise to reign over the Gentiles; in him shall the Gentiles trust," or, as it should be translated, "hope." Now, hope is ever the source of joy. So, then, in the Scriptures we see God is the God of hope, and on further search we see that the hope of the Gentiles permits them to rejoice with his people; in fine, we see that God himself is the hope of all those who know him, and the consequent source of joy and peace.

Again, then, I am brought to this, that, to begin with, the joy and peace which we all desire to obtain must be sought through a knowledge of the God of hope, as he is revealed to us by the Scriptures. We must begin with that sure word of testimony whereunto we do well if we take heed as unto a light that shineth in a dark place. There must be belief in God as revealed in the word, even though as yet we see no change within ourselves, nor any conceivable internal ground in our nature for hope or joy. Blessed is he who hath not seen and yet hath believed. He who can hang upon God without the comfort of inward experience is on the high road to being filled with joy and peace.

But the apostle in the text leads us through the Scriptures to God himself, who is personally to fill us with joy and peace; by which I understand that he is to become the great object of our joy. As Israel in the Red Sea triumphed in the Lord, even so do we joy in God by our Lord Jesus Christ. Like David, we say, "Then will I go unto the altar of God, unto God my exceeding joy"; and with Isaiah we sing, "I will greatly rejoice in the Lord; my soul shall be joyful in my God." When first the Lord looked upon us through the windows of his word we began to hope; by-and-by his good Spirit caused our hoping to grow into believing, and since then, as our knowledge of the Lord has increased, our believing has risen to fulness of joy. Our God is a blessed God, so that to believe in him is to find rest unto the soul, and to commune with him is to dwell in bliss. Beloved, when you think of God, the just one, apart from Christ, you might well tremble, but when you see him in Jesus, his very justice becomes precious to you as "the terrible crystal," and you learn to build it into the foundation of your joy. The holiness of God which aforetime awed you becomes supremely attractive when you see it revealed in the person of Jesus Christ your Lord. How charming is "the glory of God in the face of Christ." As for the love of God, as you see it set forth in this book and in his Son, it inspires you with every sacred passion. As for his eternal immutability, it becomes the groundwork of your peace, for if he changes not, then all his promises will stand sure to you and to all his people from generation to generation. His power, which was once so terrible in the thunder and in the storm, now becomes delightful to you as you see it yoked to the promise that the promise may be fulfilled, and behold it concentrated in the man Christ Jesus that his purposes may be achieved. In fine, there is no attribute of God, there is no purpose of God, there is no deed of God, there is no aspect under which God is seen, but what becomes the object of the Christian's joy when he has seen him and believed in him as revealed in the Scriptures. To the believer God is his sun, his shield, his portion, his delight, his all. His soul delights herself in the Lord. At first he hoped in God, that peradventure he would smile upon him: he turned to the Scriptures, and he found there many a cheering declaration, and these he knew to be true, and therefore he believed God that he would do as he had said; and now not only has his hope become faith, but his faith has budded and blossomed and brought forth the almonds of joy and peace. You see, then, how the Lord is the author of all our holy gladness.

Our God is, however, called the God of hope, not only because he is the object of our hope, and the ground of our joy and peace, but because he it is that worketh hope and joy in us. No joy is worth the having unless the Lord is the beginning and the end of it, and no joy is worth receiving except it springs from hope in him. He must breathe peace upon us, or else the storm-tossed waters of our spirit will never rest, nor is it desirable that they should, for peace without God is stupefaction, joy without God is madness, and hope without God is presumption.

In true believers their hope, faith, joy, and peace are all alike of divine workmanship. Our spiritual raiment is never homespun; we are divinely arrayed from head to foot.

This blessed name of "God of hope" belongs to the New Testament, and is a truly gospel title. Livy tells us that the Romans had a god of hope, but he says that the temple was struck by lightning, and in an after book he adds that it was burned to the ground. Exceedingly typical this of whatever of hope can come to nations which worship gods of their own making. All idol hopes must perish beneath the wrath of the Most High. The God of human nature unenlightened, or only sufficiently enlightened to discover its sin, is the God of terror; in fact, to many, the Lord is the God of despair: but when you turn to the revelation of God in Scripture, you find him to be a God whose gracious character inspires hope, and henceforth you turn away from everything else to fix your hope on God alone. "My soul, wait thou only upon God, for my expectation is from him." God, in Christ Jesus, has ceased to be the dread of men, and has become their hope. Our Father and our Friend, we look for all to thee. And blessed be God, the hope which he excites is a hope worthy of him. It is a God-like hope—a hope which helps us to purify ourselves. At first we hope in God for cleansing from every sin, and then for acceptance here and hereafter. We hope for pardon through the atonement which is in Christ Jesus, and when we have it, we hope for sanctification by the Spirit. Our hope never ceases to rise higher and higher, and to receive fulfilment after fulfilment, and we know that it shall continue to do so till we rise to dwell at his right hand for ever and ever. He who graspeth this hope hath a soul-satisfying portion, for which a man might well be content to suffer a thousand martyrdoms if he might but abide in it. It is a hope which only God would have contrived for man—a hope founded in himself; a hope presented to the sons of men in Christ Jesus because his sacrifice has been presented and accepted; a hope which God alone can inspire in men, for even if they hear the gospel they do not find hope till he comes in power to their souls: a hope which always adores God, and lies low at his feet, never dreaming of being independent of him; a hope which layeth her crown at his feet, and taketh him to be her Lord for ever and ever. This is the hope which is the mother of our joy and peace, and only as it is wrought in us by the Lord can we be truly happy and restful.

II. Secondly, let us enquire, WHAT IS THIS BLESSED STATE OF MIND of which we have spoken a little? Let us look into the words. He says, "That the God of hope may fill you with all joy and peace in believing." It is a state of mind most pleasant, for to be filled with joy is a rare delight, reminding one of heaven.

It is, however, a state as safe as it is pleasant, for the man who has a joy which God gives him may be quite easy in the enjoyment of it. The best of the world's joy is but for a season; while you are enjoying it you are in fear because it will soon be over, and what then? Earth's best candles will soon burn out. The day of this world's mirth will end in a night of misery. This thought mars and sours all fleeting joys; but the joy which God gives has no afterthought about it. It is wholesome and safe and abiding. We may drink our full without being sickened, yea, revel in it without surfeit.

At the same time it is most profitable joy, for the more a man has of this joy the better man he will be. It will not soften him and render him effeminate, for it has a singular strengthening power about it. There is, doubtless, a tonic influence in sorrow, but holy joy is also exceedingly invigorating, for it is written, "The joy of the Lord is your strength." The more happy we can be in our God the more thoroughly will the will of Christ be fulfilled in us, for he desired that our joy might be full. The more you rejoice in God the more you will recommend true religion. The more full of delight you are, especially in trying times, the more you will glorify God. Few things are at the same time both pleasant and profitable, but holy joy and peace possess that double excellence. Fulness of spiritual joy is both the index and the means of spiritual strength. I commend this state, therefore, to you. I trust that we shall not be so unbelieving as to be afraid of heaven's own consolations, nor so unreasonable as to decline to be filled with joy and peace when they may be had by believing.

Now, notice, that it is a state which has varieties in it. It is joy and peace; and it may be either. Sometimes the believer is full of joy. Joy is active and expressive; it sparkles and flashes like a diamond; it sings and dances like David before the ark. To be filled with holy joy is a delicious excitement of the sweetest kind; may you often experience it, until strangers are compelled to infer that the Lord hath done great things for you. Nevertheless, the flesh is weak, and might hardly endure continuous delight, and so there comes a relief, in the lovely form of peace, in which the heart is really joyous, but after a calm and quiet manner. I have seen the ringers make the pinnacles of a church tower reel to and fro while they have made the joy bells sound out to the full, and then they have played quietly, and let the fabric settle down again. Even thus does joy strain the man, but peace comes in to give him rest. In this peace there is not much to exhilarate, not much which could fittingly be spoken out in song; but silence, full of infinite meaning, becomes the floodgate of the soul. You seek not the exulting assembly, but the calm shade and the quiet chamber. You are as happy as you were in your joy, but not so stirred and moved. Peace is joy resting, and joy is peace dancing. Joy cries hosanna before the Well-beloved, but peace leans her head on his bosom. In the midst of bereavements and sickness we may scarcely be able to rejoice, but we may be at peace. When faith cannot break through a troop with her sacred joy she stands still and sees the salvation of God in hallowed peace. We work with joy and rest with peace. What a blessing it is that when we come to die if we cannot depart with the banners of triumphant joy all flying in the breeze, we can yet fall asleep safely in the arms of peace. How pleasant a life do they lead who are not the subjects of any very great excitement, but maintain calm and quiet communion with God. Their heart is fixed, trusting in the Lord. They neither soar nor sink, but keep the even tenor of their way. It is a state of mind, then, which admits of variations; and I really do not know which to choose out of its two forms. I should not like to be without joy, and yet methinks there is something so solid about peace that I might almost give it the preference. I think I love the quiet sister the better of the two. That famous text in Isaiah—"They shall mount up with wings as eagles; they shall run, and not be weary; and they shall walk and not faint" looks somewhat like an anti-climax; it would appear to place the greatest first, and then the less, and then the least; but it is not so. The mounting up with wings as eagles must always be more or less temporary: we are not eagles, and cannot always be on the wing. The Lord renews our strength like the eagles, and this shows we are not always up to the eagle mark. Well, though it is a grand thing to be able to fly, it is a better thing to be able to run; this is more like a man, involves less danger, and is more practically useful. It is good to run, but even that is not the best journey pace: it is best of all to walk, for this is a steady, persevering pace to move at. "Enoch walked with God." This is God's pace, who even when he makes clouds his chariot is described as walking upon the wings of the wind. We read of the walk of faith, and the walk of holiness, for walking is practical, and is meant for every day. You young people, I like to see you run, and I am glad to take a turn at it myself, but, after all, steady, sober, unwearied walking is the best. To walk without fainting is a high experimental attainment, and is none the less valuable because at first sight there seems nothing striking about it. Walking is the emblem of peace, and running and mounting up with wings as eagles are the emblems of joy.

But, beloved, this blessed state is also a compound, for we are bidden at one and the same time to receive both wine and milk—wine exhilarating with joy, and milk satisfying with peace. "Ye shall go out with joy, and be led forth with peace." You shall lie down in the green pastures of delight, and be led by the still waters of quietness. Our heart may be as an ocean, gloriously casting upward its spray of joy, and lifting up its waves on high in delight, as one clappeth his hands for joy; and yet, at the same time, as down deep in the coral caverns all is still and undisturbed, so may the heart be quiet as a sleeping babe. We see no difficulty in understanding both lines of the hymn—

> "My heart is resting, O my God,
> I will give thanks and sing."

We rest and praise, as trees hold to the earth by their roots, and perfume the air with their bloom; as morning comes without sound of trumpet, and yet awakens the music of birds by its arising. Ours is no froth of joy; there is solid peace beneath our effervescence of delight. Happy are we to have learned how to combine two such choice things.

> "Joy is a fruit that will not grow
>   In nature's barren soil;
> All we can boast, till Christ we know,
>   Is vanity and toil.
> "But where the Lord has planted grace,
>   And made his glories known,
> These fruits of heavenly joy and peace
>   Are found, and there alone."

Now, I want you to lay stress on the next observation I am about to make, because I began with it, and wish to leave it upon your minds as the chief thought. The joy and peace here spoken of are through believing. You come to know the God of hope through the Scriptures, which reveal him; by this you are led to believe in him, and it is through that believing that you become filled with joy and peace. It is not by working, nor by feeling, that we become full of joy; our peace does not arise from the marks, and evidences, and experiences which testify to us that we are the sons of God, but simply from believing. Our central joy and peace must always come to us, not as an inference from the internal work of the Spirit in our souls, but from the finished work of the Lord Jesus, and the promises of God contained in the Scriptures. We must continue to look out of self to the written word wherein the Lord is set forth before us, and we must rest in God in Christ Jesus as the main basis of our hope; not depending upon any other arguments than those supplied by the Bible itself. I will show by-and-by how we shall afterwards reach to a hope which flows out of the work of the Spirit within us; but at the first, and, I think, permanently and continuously, the main ground of the surest joy and truest peace must come to us through simply believing in Jesus Christ. Beloved, I know that I have been converted, for I am sure that there is a change of heart in me; nevertheless, my hope of eternal life does not hang upon the inward fact. I rest in the external fact that God hath revealed himself in Jesus as blotting out the sin of all his believing people, and, as a believer, I have the word of God as my guarantee of forgiveness. This is my rest. Because I am a believer in Christ Jesus, therefore have I hope, therefore have I joy and peace, since God hath declared that "he that believeth in him hath everlasting life." This joy can only safely come through believing, and I pray you, brothers and sisters, never be drifted away from child-like faith in what God hath said. It is very easy to obtain a temporary joy and peace through your present easy experience, but how will you do when all things within take a troublous turn? Those who live by feeling change with the weather. If you ever put aside your faith in the finished work to drink from the cup of your own inward sensations, you will find yourself bitterly disappointed. Your honey will turn to gall, your sunshine into blackness; for all things which come of man are fickle and deceptive. The God of hope will fill you with joy and peace, but it will only be through believing. You will still have to stand as a poor sinner at the foot of the cross, trusting to the complete atonement. You will never have joy and peace unless you do. If you once begin to say, "I am a saint; there is something good in me," and so on, you will find joy evaporate and peace depart. Hold on to your believing.

Come back to the text again, and you will find that this joy and peace, according to Paul, are of a superlative character, for, after his manner, Paul makes language for himself. He often manufactures a superlative by the use of the word "all," as here, "Fill you with all joy." He means with the best and highest degree of joy, with as much joy as you can hold, with the very choicest and most full of joys in earth or in heaven. God give you the joy of joys, the light of delight, the heaven of heaven.

Then notice the comprehensiveness of his prayer. "All joy"; that is joy in God the Father's love, joy in God the Son's redeeming blood, joy in God the Holy Ghost's indwelling; joy in the covenant of grace, joy in the seal and witness of it, joy in the promises, joy in the decrees, joy in the doctrines, joy in the precepts, joy in everything which cometh from God, "all joy." Paul also requests for them all peace, peace with God, peace of conscience, peace with one another, peace even with the outside world, as far as peace may be. May you all have it.

And now observe the degree of joy and peace which he wishes for them—"that ye may be filled," and that by the God of hope himself. God alone knows our capacity and where the vacuum lies which most needs filling. A man might try to fill us and fail, but God, who made us, knows every corner and cranny of our nature, and can pour in joy and peace till every portion of our being is flooded, saturated, and overflowed with delight. I like to remember David's word, "The rain also filleth the pools," for even thus doth the Lord pour his grace upon the thirsty soil of our hearts till it stands in pools. As the sun fills the world with light, and enters into all places, even so the God of hope by his presence lights up every part of our nature with the golden light of joyous peace, till there is not a corner left for sadness or foreboding. This is Paul's prayer, and he expects its answer to come to us through believing, and in no other way; he does not ask for us mysterious revelations, dreams, visions, or presumptuous persuasions; he seeks for us no excitement of fanaticism nor the intoxication of great crowds and pleasing oratory, neither does he seek that we may imagine ourselves to be perfect, and all that kind of lumber, but that we may be happy through simply believing in the God of hope as he is set forth in the Bible. I take this book of God into my hands and say, "Whatsoever things are written here were written for my learning, that through patience and comfort of the Scriptures I might have hope"; I do have hope, for I believe this book, and now I feel joy and peace welling up within my soul.

Brethren, receive ye this benediction! O Lord, fulfil it in the heart of every believer before thee.

III. Now thirdly, WHAT DOES THIS LEAD TO? "Lead to?" says one, "Lead to, why surely it is enough in itself. What more is wanted?" When a man brings you into a chamber vaulted with diamonds and amethysts, and pearls and rubies; with walls composed of slabs of gold, and the floor made of solid pavements of silver, we should be astonished if he said, "This is a passage to something richer still." Yet the apostle directs us to this fulness of joy and peace through believing that we may by its means reach to something else,—"that you may abound in hope through the power of the Holy Ghost." How often do great things in the Bible, like the perpetual cycles of nature, begin where they end and end where they begin. If we begin with the God of hope, we are wound up into holy joy and peace, that we may come back to hope again and to abounding in it by the power of the Holy Ghost.

First, I notice that the hope here mentioned arises, not out of pure believing, but out of the joy created in us by our having believed. Hope led to faith, faith to joy, and now joy back again to hope. This is the story as far as I am concerned:—I began with believing. I felt nothing good within me, but I believed in what God revealed concerning himself. I saw nothing, but I believed, on the ground that God said so. I soon had joy and peace in my soul as the result of my faith, and now, because of this joy and peace, I hope and expect further blessings. Though still resting my soul upon the finished work of Jesus, yet hopes do arise from the work of the Holy Ghost within me. The

God who has given me by believing to rejoice that the past is all atoned for, and who has given me peace because my sins are forgiven me for his name's sake, will not dash that joy by revoking my pardon. He who has given me joy, because he has quickened me, and has, up to this day, preserved me, will not, I am persuaded, forsake me, and suffer me to perish. Surely he will never leave me, after having done so much for me. My present joy gives me a hope, most sure and steadfast, that he will never turn his back upon me. If he did not intend to bless me in the future, he would not have done so much for me in the past, and he could not and would not be doing so much for me now.

This hope, you perceive, drinks its life at the fountain of personal experience. The first hope we ever know comes together with our simply believing the word of God, but now there arises in us an abounding of hope, which is the outgrowth of the inward life. Fear is banished now, for we have looked to the God of hope, and found acceptance in the Beloved. Now, therefore, in the chamber where fear formerly dwelt hope takes up its habitation; azure-winged, bright-eyed hope makes its nest there, and sings to us all the day long.

The text speaks of an abounding hope, and if you consider for awhile you will see that very much hope must arise to a Christian out of his spiritual joy. If you have once been in the bosom of Jesus, and known his joy, your hope will overflow. For instance, you will argue—he has pardoned my sin, and made me to rejoice as a forgiven man: will he condemn me after all? What meaneth the pardon if, after all, the transgressions are to be laid upon me, and I am to suffer for my sin? The believer hath great joy because God's love is shed abroad in his soul, and he argues that if the Lord loves him so intensely now, he will not undergo a change, and remove his love. He who in love redeemed me by the blood of his Son will love me eternally, for he changes not. Is not this sound argument? Grace enjoyed is a pledge of glory. Redeeming love is the guarantee of preserving love. Acceptance with God to-day creates a blessed hope of acceptance for ever. Faith and joy within the soul sing to one another somewhat after this fashion:—

> "His smiles have freed my heart from pain,
>   My drooping spirits cheer'd;
> And will he not appear again
>   Where he has once appeared?
> "Has he not form'd my soul anew,
>   And caused my light to shine;
> And will he now his work undo,
>   Or break his word divine?"

Perfectly assured of the Lord's goodness, the man confronts the future without fear, and in due time approaches death without dismay. Since the Lord has begun to make us like his Son we conclude that he will perfect his work, and raise us from our graves in the full image of our Redeemer. He has given us already to know something of the joy of Christ, who prayed that his joy might be fulfilled in us that our joy might be full, and therefore we are sure that we shall bask in the joy of heaven. We will, therefore, lie down in peace, and rest when our last day on earth shall come, for we shall rise with Jesus: of this we have no doubt. We shall enter into the joy of the Lord, for we have entered into it already. Thus out of peace and joy there grow the noblest of human hopes. Little enjoyment, like a weak telescope, gives us but a faint prospect, but great enjoyment is an optic glass of marvellous power, and brings great things near to us. Joy and peace are specimens of heaven's felicities, and set the soul both hoping and hungering. Having tasted of the grapes of Eshcol, we believe in the land which floweth with milk and honey, and long to rest under the boughs which bear such luscious clusters. We have seen the celestial city far away, but the light of it is so surpassing that we have longed to walk its golden streets, ay, and have felt sure of doing so ere long. He who has seen a little of the light of the morning expects the more eagerly the noonday. He who has waded into the river of joy up to the ankles, becomes eager to enter it still further, till he finds it a river to swim in, wherein the soul is borne along by a sacred current of unutterable delight. Up, ye saints, to your Pisgah of joy, for there you shall have a full view of Canaan which stretches before you, and is soon to be yours. Whatever your joy and peace may be now you ought to see at once that they are meant to be only a platform from which you are to look for something brighter and better still: ye are filled with joy and peace that ye may abound in hope.

Our apostle rightly adds, "by the power of the Holy Ghost," for I take it that this is partly mentioned by way of caution, because there are hopes arising out of inward experience which may turn out to be fallacious, and therefore we must discriminate between the hope of nature and the hope of grace. I have heard young people say, "I know I am saved, because I am so happy." Be not too sure of that. Many people think themselves very happy, and yet they are not saved. The world has a happiness which is a fatal sign, and a peace which is the token of spiritual death. Discernment, therefore, is needed lest we mistake the calm before a storm for the rest which the Lord giveth to those who come unto him. Hope may arise out of our joy, but we must mind that we do not fix our confidence in it, or we shall have a sandy foundation. The solid grace of hope which abides and remains in the soul is born of faith through the word; it is only the abounding of hope which comes out of our joy and peace. Let me begin again with you lest there should be any mistake. You hear of the God of hope, and are led to believe in God as he is revealed in Scripture. So far all is plain sailing. If you believe in the Christ of God, you obtain joy and peace, but these are results, not causes: you must not begin with your own joy and peace, and say, "My hope of salvation is built upon the happiness I have felt of late." This will never do. Begin first of all with the Scriptures, not with your feelings or fancies, nor with your impressions and excitements: these will be ruinous as a foundation. Begin with God revealed in Christ Jesus as the God of hope, and let your joy and your peace come from your believing in him: then afterwards it will be fair enough to draw arguments for the aboundings of hope, but it must be by the Holy Ghost. That hope which is worth having, which springs from inward experience, must still be wrought in us by the Holy Spirit, and I will show you how it is natural that it should be so. We ask ourselves, "How shall I hold on to the end?" The answer will be suggested by another question, "How have I held on till now?" I feel now a joy and peace because my faith has been sustained until this day, how have I been preserved hitherto? By the Holy Spirit. Then he is able to keep me to the end. I feel joy and peace already, because in some measure sin is conquered in me. How will my soul be yet further sanctified and sin cast out of me? Why, by the same Holy Spirit, who has already renewed me. I have have had an earnest of what he can do, and therefore I have an abounding of hope of what he will do. My joyful experience of his indwelling, comforting, illuminating, and sanctifying power leads me into a full and confident assurance that he will carry on the work of grace, and present me complete at the last great day.

Beloved, go forward, keeping close to the groundwork of faith, and you will feel joy and peace in your hearts. At such times give full play to your hope. Expect what you will. "Eye hath not seen, nor ear heard, neither have entered into the heart of man, the things which God hath prepared for them that love him." Expect great things, expect things beyond all expectation. Your largest hopes shall all be exceeded. Hope, and hope, and yet hope again, and each time hope more and more, but the Lord will give you more than you have hoped for. When you enter his palace gates at the last, you will say, "My imagination never conceived it, my desires never compassed it, my hope never expected it; the glory surpasses all. The tenth hath not been told me of the things which God had provided for me." "Rejoice in the Lord alway: and again I say, rejoice." Amen.

6

PLEADING FOR PRAYER (1886)

"Now I beseech you, brethren, for the Lord Jesus Christ's sake, and for the love of the Spirit, that ye strive together with me in your prayers to God for me; that I may be delivered from them that do not believe in Judæa; and that my service which I have for Jerusalem may be accepted of the saints; that I may come unto you with joy by the will of God, and may with you be refreshed. Now the God of peace be with you all. Amen."—Romans 15:30–33.

"What did Paul do when his spirit was greatly oppressed?

He wrote to his brethren to pray for him."

—

THE apostle of the Gentiles held a very useful and glorious office; but he had by no means a smooth path in life. When we read the account of his sufferings, and persecutions, and labours, we wonder how a single individual could have gone through them all. He was a true hero: though a Hebrew of the Hebrews, he stands in the very front of the whole Gentile church as its founder and teacher under God, and we owe to him what we can never fully estimate. When we consider the struggles of his life, we do not wonder that the apostle was sometimes in great sorrow of heart, and heavily burdened in spirit. He was so at the time when he wrote this Epistle to the Christian friends at Rome. It was a great delight to him to have to go to Jerusalem—it was a place which was much reverenced and loved by him; it was a greater privilege for him to go and exchange salutations with his brother apostles; and it was the most joyous privilege of all to be the bearer of a contribution from the Gentiles to relieve the necessities of the saints at Jerusalem. He rejoiced much more in that gift to Jewish believers than if it had been anything for himself. But he was well aware that there were those in Judæa who hated him with deadly hatred, and would seek his life. He had been the rising hope of the Jewish party, and he had become a Christian; therefore the bigoted Jews regarded him as an apostate from the faith of their fathers. They had, moreover, a special venom against him, since he was more bold than any other Christian teacher in going among the Gentiles, and shaking off altogether the bonds of the ceremonial law; he also came out more clearly than any other man upon the doctrines of grace, and salvation by the cross of Christ, and this provoked the fiercest hostility. Paul had also the apprehension that he would not be well received even by the brethren at Jerusalem. He knew what a strong conservative feeling there was among the circumcision for the maintenance of the old Jewish law, and how he was a marked man because he had shaken off entirely that yoke of bondage. Thus he had fears as to foes, and doubts about friends. His case was peculiarly hard.

What did Paul do when his spirit was greatly oppressed? He wrote to his brethren to pray for him. He asked the good friends at Rome that they would lift up their hearts earnestly and unitedly to God, that he might be preserved from the double evil which threatened him. In the last chapter of this epistle we have the names of a great many of those private individuals at Rome to whom the apostle appealed. We do not know any of them, except it be Priscilla and Aquila, of whom we have heard elsewhere; but this great man, this inspired apostle of God, who was not a whit behind the very chief of Christ's servants, makes his appeal to these unknown and humble individuals, that they would strive together with him in their prayers. I delight in this; it shows the lowly spirit of the apostle Paul, and it reveals to us his high value for the prayers of obscure men and women. He feels that he needs what the prayers of these people can bring to him; he is sure that without those prayers he will be in danger of failure, but that with them he will be strong for his great enterprise. He sees what prayer can do, and he would arouse it into powerful action.

Does it astonish you that a man so rich in grace as Paul should be asking prayers of these unknown saints? It need not astonish you; for it is the rule with the truly great to think most highly of others. In proportion as a man grows in grace he feels his dependence upon God, and, in a certain sense, his dependence upon God's people. He decreases in his own esteem, and his brethren increase in his estimation. A flourishing tradesman, a man who has a large business, is the man who needs others, he prospers by setting others to labour on his behalf; the larger his trade, the more he is dependent upon those around him. The apostle was, so to speak, a great master-trader for the Lord Jesus; he did a great business for his Lord, and he felt that he could not carry it on unless he had the co-operation of many helpers. He did not so much want what employers harshly call "hands" to work for him, but he did need hearts to plead for him, and he therefore sent all the way to Rome to seek such assistance. He wrote to those whom he had never seen, and begged their prayers, as if he pleaded for his life. The great apostle entreats Tryphena and Tryphosa, and Mary and Julia, to pray for him. His great enterprise needs their supplications. In a great battle the general's name is mentioned; but what could he have done without the common soldiers? Wellington will always be associated with Waterloo; but, after all, it was a soldiers' battle. What could the commander have done if those in the ranks had failed him? The commander-in-chief might very well have touched his hat to the least subaltern or to the humblest private, and have said, "I thank you, comrade. Without you we could not have conquered." The chief troubles of the great day of Waterloo arose from certain very doubtful allies, who wavered in the hour of battle—those were the general's weakness; but his hope and strength lay in those regiments which were as an iron wall against the enemy. Even thus the faithful are our joy and crown; but the unstable are our sorrow and weakness. Every ministering servant of the Lord Jesus Christ is in much the same condition as Paul: true, we are of a lower grade, and our work is on a smaller scale; but our needs are just as great. We have not all the grace which Paul possessed; but for that very reason we make the more pathetic an appeal to you, our friends and fellow-helpers, while we use the apostle's language, and cry, "We beseech you, brethren, for the Lord Jesus Christ's sake, and for the love of the Spirit, that ye strive together with us in your prayers to God for us."

I shall call your attention to this text with the longing in my own heart that I may more abundantly myself live in your prayers. I have to rejoice in the prayers of thousands of holy men and women who love me in the Lord. I am deeply grateful for the affectionate supplications of multitudes whom I have not seen in the flesh, to whom the printed sermons go week by week. I am a debtor, not only to the beloved people around me, but to a larger company all over the world. These are my comfort, my riches, my strength. To such I speak at this time. Beloved, I need your prayers more than ever. I am more and more conscious of their value; do not restrain them. Just now there is to me a special need of grace on many accounts, and I hope that some of those who have long borne me up will give me a special portion of aid at this hour. I am not worthy to use the same language as the apostle Paul, but I know no better, and my necessity is even greater than his: therefore I borrow his words, and say, "I beseech you, brethren, for the Lord Jesus Christ's sake, and for the love of the Spirit, that ye strive together with me in your prayers to God for me."

In our text there are two things: prayer asked, and a blessing given—"Now the God of peace be with you all. Amen."

I. First, here is PRAYER ASKED FOR.

We will look at the apostle's request for prayer in general, and then afterwards we will look to the details which are mentioned in the thirty-first verse.

First, here is a request to the people of God for prayer in general. He asks it for himself—"That ye strive together with me in your prayers to God for me." He knew his own weakness, he knew the difficulty of the work to which he had been called, he knew that if he failed in his enterprise it would be a sad failure, injurious through coming ages to the entire church. He cried, "Agonize for me," because he felt that much depended upon him. It is like a man who is willing to lead the forlorn hope; but he says to his comrades, "You will support me." It is like one who is willing to go into a far country, bearing his life in his hands; but he plaintively exclaims, "You won't forget me, will you? Though you stay at home, you will think of me!" It reminds us of Carey, who says, when he goes to India, "I will go down into the pit, but brother Fuller and the rest of you must hold the rope." Can we refuse the request? Would it not be treachery? It is not according to the heart of true yoke-fellows, it is not according to the instincts of our common humanity, that we should desert any man whom we set in the front of the battle. If we choose a man to be our representative in the service of our God, we will not desert him. A man cannot be charged with egotism if he begs for personal support when he is engaged in labours for others, and is not seeking himself but the success of the great cause. Under heavy responsibilities he does well to enlist the sympathies and prayers of those whom he is serving; and he has a right to have them. Beloved friends, if you are with me in the great battle for

God and truth, and if you count me worthy to bear the brunt of this war, I beseech you for Christ's sake support me by your importunate wrestlings at the throne of grace. Pray for all ministers and workers, but pray also for me. I am of all men the most miserable if you deny me this.

Observe in what relationship he regards them when he puts the request. "Now," saith he," I beseech you, brethren." "I beseech you." It is the strongest word of entreaty he can find. It is as if he said, "I go down on my knees to you, and implore you. I ask it of you as the greatest favour you can do me. I ask it of you as the dearest token of your love, that you strive together with me in your prayers to God for me." He does not call them companions, or fellow-workers, or friends; but he addresses them as brothers. "You are my brethren," saith he; "I feel a love to you, you Romans, converted to God. I have a longing in my heart to see you; and though I have not so much as spoken with you face to face, yet we are brothers. The life that is in you beats also in my heart; we are born again of the same Father, we are quickened by the same Spirit, we are redeemed by the same Saviour, therefore, spiritually, we are brethren. Shall not brothers pray for one another? He seems to say, "If ye be brethren, show this token of your brotherhood. You cannot go up with me to Jerusalem, and share my danger, but you can be with me in spirit, and by your prayers surround me with divine protection. I do not ask you to come, ye Romans, with your swords and shields, and make a body-guard about me; but I do beg of you, my true brothers, if you be so indeed, to agonize together with me in your prayers to God for me." If there remains in the Christian church any brotherhood whatsoever, every leader of the host, every preacher of the gospel, every pastor of a church, should receive the proof of that brotherhood in the shape of daily intercession. Every sent servant of God beseeches his brethren that they strive together with him in prayer to God for him; and I am not a whit behind any of them in the urgency of my request to the many who have hitherto proved themselves my brethren. I know your love has not grown cold to me: I have abundant evidence of that. O my brothers, act as brothers to me now, and beseech the Lord to bless me.

But observe what kind of prayer he asks for: "That ye strive together,"—that ye "agonize,"—that is the word. You have before you in this expression a reminder of that great agony in Gethsemane, and I should think the apostle had that picture before his eyes. In the garden our Lord not only prayed as was his wont, but with strong crying and tears he made his appeal to God. "Being in an agony he prayed more earnestly." He wrestled till he "sweat as it were great drops of blood falling down to the ground," but none agonized together with him. That was one of the deepest shades of the picture, that he must tread the wine-press alone, and of the people there must be none with him. Yet did our Lord seem to ask for sympathy and help.

> "Backward and forward thrice he ran,
> As if he sought some help from man";

but he found none even to watch with him one hour, much less to agonize with him. The apostle felt that an agony alone was too bitter for him, and he therefore piteously cries, "I beseech you, brethren, that ye agonize with me in prayer to God for me." Now, as the disciples ought to have sympathized with the Saviour, and entered into his direful grief, but did not, even so it may happen to us. But, brethren, I trust that the unfaithfulness to the Master will not be repeated upon his servants. It remains to all that are true brethren in Christ that, when they see a man in agony of heart for Christ's sake and for souls' sake, they should bow the knee side by side with him, and be true brothers to him. When his labours become intense, when his difficulties are multiplied, when his heart begins to sink, and his strength is failing him, then the man must wrestle with his God, then his brethren must wrestle at his side. When the uplifted hands of Moses are known to bring a blessing, Aaron and Hur must stay them up when they are seen to grow weary. When Jacob is struggling at Jabbok, and we see him there, we must turn in and help him to detain the angel of the covenant. If one man can hold him fast by saying, "I will not let thee go unless thou bless me," surely a score of you can make a cordon round about him, and speedily win the blessing. What may not a hundred do? Let us try the power of agonizing prayer! Do we know as yet what it means? Let us rise as one man and cry, "O angel, whose hands are full of benedictions, we will not let thee go, except thou give us thine own blessing; the blessing of thy covenant." If two of you are agreed as touching anything concerning the kingdom, you shall be heard; but what if hundreds and thousands of the faithful are of one mind and one mouth in this matter? Will you not at once cry unto God, "Bless thou thy servants; establish thou the work of our hands upon us; yea, the work of our hands establish thou it"? You see it is earnest prayer which Paul asks for, not the prayer which foams itself away in words; but prayer with force, with energy, with humble boldness, with intensity of desire, with awful earnestness; prayer which, like a deep, hidden torrent, cuts a channel even through a rock. His request was "that ye wrestle with me in your prayers to God for me"; and this is our request this day.

He does not, however, wish for a single moment to exclude himself from the prayer; for he says, "that ye agonize with me." He is to be the first agonizer. This should be the position of every minister. We ought to be examples of wrestling prayer. How I wish that you could realize more fully the work allotted to the apostles when they said that it was not reason that they should leave the word of God to serve tables! There was a difference about the distribution of the alms-money among the widows, and the twelve declared that they could not attend to such a matter; for, said they, "We will give ourselves continually to prayer and to the ministry of the word." This would be heaven to me. But notice that at least half, and the first half, of their work lay in prayer. Oh, if that could be our portion! If we could but have full space for prayer and meditation, and were set free from the petty secularities and differences incident to church life. Oh that we could have more to do with him from whose right hand the supreme blessing comes—that were a joy indeed! But even if the apostle could thus himself agonize, he did not feel satisfied; for he beseeches others to wrestle with him in prayer to God. He sought communion in supplication. Even thus would I beseech you, brethren, to come with me into the inner chamber. Come with me into the holy of holies; let us together approach the mercy-seat. Lend me the help of all the spiritual force you have, that we may together agonize in prayer to God, that the blessing may descend upon the enterprises now in my hands. You see the sort of prayer which is needed, even the effectual fervent prayer of righteous men; and may the Holy Spirit brace up our spirits, that we may be able to join in such agonizing in this time of need.

This verse is one of the most intense I ever remember to have read, even in so intense a book as this Holy Scripture. Observe the fervency of the pleading—"Now I beseech you, brethren, for the Lord Jesus Christ's sake." What an argument! That name is full of power with true hearts. You owe him everything, you owe him your souls, you owe him every hope for the future, every comfort in the present, and every happy memory of the past. Your life would have been worse than death apart from him. His love to you constrains you, because you thus judge, that when one died for all, all died, and that you so died that henceforth you should not live unto yourselves but unto him. Now, saith he, as you cannot repay the Lord Jesus Christ personally, repay it to his servant by your prayers; join him in his agony in recollection of that greater agony in which none could join, by which you were redeemed from death and hell. If there be any love to Christ in a Christian's heart he must pray that the Holy Spirit would bless the ministry of the word. Surely your hearts must be turned to stone if you do not plead for a blessing upon that ministry by which you yourselves have been brought to Christ. If I have been a spiritual father to any of you, you will not fail to pray for me. Will you? As you love that Saviour whom I preach, I beseech you, for the sake of Jesus Christ, that ye strive together with me in your prayers to God for me.

But he adds to that another argument—"for the love of the Spirit." If the Spirit of God has indeed loved you and proved it by quickening and sanctifying you, then pray for his ministers. If the Spirit of God has created a love in you, which is stronger than mere natural affection,—a love which does not arise out of any fleshly relationship, or any mere association, or any casual partiality, but a love which the Holy Spirit himself creates and fosters in your heart— then pray for me. If there be such love in you, not natural and temporary, but spiritual and therefore everlasting, then pray for the Lord's servant. If there be in you a love which may exist, nay, will exist, in heaven itself; if there be such a love in you, then saith the apostle, I beseech you, pray for me. Brethren, I say the same. Unless our profession is a lie we love each other, and we must therefore show that love by our prayers for one another. Especially if any of you have been brought to the Lord Jesus Christ by the ministry of any man whom God favours with his help, then that man must live for ever in your hearts, and be remembered in your prayers. You cannot escape from the obligation of intercession for the man who brought you to Jesus. As long as you live, and as long as he remains faithful, you must bear him on your heart in supplication. It must be so: the love of the Spirit has knit us to one another, and none can put us asunder. Ours is no feigned unity, but deep, and true, and real. In Christ Jesus, my brother, there has been begotten in our hearts an affection for one another which death itself shall not destroy. We will not be separated. Then, by the love of the Spirit, I beseech you that ye

131

agonize together with me in your prayers to God for me. Every word pleads with tears: there is not a waste letter in the whole verse.

Why do you think the apostle at that special time asked these brethren to pray for him so? Was it not because he believed in the providence of God? He was going up to Jerusalem, and the Jews would seek to slay him. They hunted him in every place, and now he was going into the lion's den; but he believed that God in Providence could overrule all things, so that he should not suffer injury at the hands of blood-thirsty zealots; but should be delivered out of their malicious power. We also believe in God that worketh all things; therefore, let us pray that all opposition to his gospel may be overcome.

He believed also in the influence that God can have upon men's hearts, especially upon the hearts of his own people. He was afraid that the Jewish believers would be very cold to him, and therefore he prays God that his Holy Spirit may warm their hearts, and make them full of love, so that the offerings he took to them from the Grecian churches might be accepted, and might foster a sense of hearty fellowship in the hearts of the Hebrew saints towards their Gentile brethren. Do you not also believe that the hearts of all men are in the hands of the Lord? Do you not believe in the supremacy of the will of God over the freewill of man? Do you not rejoice that there is not only a Providence that shapes our ends, but a secret influence which moulds men's hearts? Therefore it is that we urge you to plead with God that we also may have acceptance with his people. We desire to render them much service, and to enjoy their loving regard. It is painful to us to differ with any, and joyous to be in communion with all parts of the church of our Lord Jesus Christ.

What is more than this, the apostle believed in the power of the prayers of simple people so to move the mind of God that he would exert his hand in providence and his influence over the hearts of men. Never let us imagine that the doctrine of the fixity of events, or the supremacy of law, as the philosophers call it, is at all contrary to the truth that prayer is effectual for its own ends and purposes. In olden times a warrior was going forth to battle for his country, and a certain preacher of the word said to him, "My prayer is made continually for you that you may be victorious." The warrior, in his philosophic doubt, replied that he saw no use in the promised prayers; for if God had determined to give him victory, he would have it without prayer; and if fate had decreed that he should be defeated, prayers could not prevent it. To which the godly man very properly replied, "Then take off your helmet and your coat of mail, and hang up your sword and buckler. Go not forth to battle at all with your men-at-arms; for, indeed, if the Lord is to conquer your enemies he can do it without your weapons, and if he will not prosper you, it is in vain for you to mount your war-horse." The argument, when carried out, answers itself: there is, in truth, no force in it. The net result of such reasoning would be absolute inaction. Common sense shows us how absurd it is. All means are to be used, notwithstanding the eternal purpose of God; for that purpose includes means and their uses. We declare that among the most potent means in all the world is prayer; and this must not be neglected. There are certain ascertained forces, and among those forces, always to be reckoned with and relied upon, is the force of the cry of God's dear children to their great Father in heaven; in other words, the power of prayer. In prayer we present the sacrifice of God's own Son to God's own self, and prevail by its means. O brothers and sisters, we ask your prayers without doubt or question. We know and are persuaded that they will avail much. By your power in prayer God's power will be set in motion, and by that force all will be accomplished which shall be for his glory and for our good.

I hope you have been so far interested; may God grant you may have been influenced by these remarks, and excited to incessant intercession!

In our text there is, in the next place, a statement of the apostle's desires in detail. When we pray, we should make a point of praying for something distinctly. There is a general kind of praying, which fails from want of precision. It is as if a regiment of soldiers should all fire off their guns anyhow; possibly somebody would be killed, but the majority of the enemy would be missed. I believe that at the battle of Waterloo, there were no arms of precision, they had only the old Brown Bess, and though the battle was won, it has been said that it took as much lead to kill a man as the weight of the man's body. This is a figure of the comparative failure of indistinct, generalizing prayer. If you pray anyhow, if it be with sincerity, a measure of blessing results from it; but it will take a great deal of such praying to accomplish much. But if you plead for certain mercies definitely and distinctly, with firm unstaggering faith, you shall richly succeed.

Our apostle gives his friends three things to pray for: First, he would have them ask that he might be delivered from them that did not believe in Judæa. He was delivered, not perhaps in the precise manner which he hoped for; but he was to the letter delivered from the unbelieving Jews. Certain zealots bound themselves with an oath that they would not eat till they had slain him; but they went a long while hungry; for the arm of the Roman Empire was stretched forth to protect Paul against his infuriated countrymen. Strange it was that Cæsar's power must be as a shield around the feeble servant of the mighty God! From raging mobs and secret confederacies Paul was saved, apparently, by Roman soldiers, but secretly by Roman saints. Against all oppositions from without let us pray.

They were also to ask of the Lord that his service which he had for Jerusalem might be accepted of the saints. This also was granted; the brethren did accept Paul's embassy. He met with little difficulty; the contribution was accepted with much gratitude, and we do not hear afterwards of those bickerings between the Jewish and the Gentile believers. Much was done in the apostolic college at Jerusalem to create a heartier feeling towards the Gentile brethren, and the kingdom of Christ henceforth owned to be over all races and kindreds of men. Paul did accomplish very much, and had comfort in his mission to the mother church. Oh that we also could be of service to that community of Christians to which we belong!

Brethren, pray that our word may be accepted of our own brethren; for some of these are wandering from the way of truth.

They were to pray next, that he might come unto them with joy by the will of God; and might, with them, be refreshed. That was to be the third prayer. It is to be observed that this petition also was heard, but it was not answered as Paul might have expected or desired. He did come to them according to the will of God rather than by his own will. He may or may not have been on his way to Spain, as he purposed: he certainly was on his way to prison, as he had not purposed. His first prayer, that he might be delivered from them that believe not in Judæa, was not answered in the way of his never being in danger from them, or coming into difficulties through them; but he was delivered out of their hands by becoming a prisoner to the Roman governor, and being sent under his guardianship to Cæsar, to whom he had appealed. By that means he travelled to Rome at the expense of the Imperial Government, and on landing at Puteoli, close to Naples, he found friends waiting for him; and as soon as the Roman brethren heard of his landing, they despatched a company to meet him at Appii. Forum, a place on the road to Rome, where they stopped to change horses, and to take refreshments. There he saw his prayer beginning to be answered. Further on, at a place called the Three Taverns, more dear friends from Rome met him, "whom when Paul saw, he thanked God, and took courage." The Roman saints had long looked for the apostle, and he came at last—an ambassador in bonds, a prisoner who must go to the Prætorian guard-room, and there await the emperor's will and pleasure. They had not expected to see him in such case; but they were not ashamed of his chain. They made a considerable journey to meet him, and he was filled with their company, and refreshed by their fellowship, as he had desired. Even his imprisonment may have been a rest for him; it could not have involved such wear and tear as his former labours and persecutions. We read the other day that Holloway Gaol is a choice place for rest and enjoyment to a man with a clear conscience; and I dare say that Paul found his confinement at Rome to be rather a refreshment than otherwise after his years of weariness and buffetings. There he was shut away from his furious persecutors; certainly, no Jew could take his there. He was not afraid of being stoned while in imperial custody; and probably he was the more at ease because he had not to preach to such as the Corinthians and the Galatians, from whom he had asked no prayers, but had received much grief. He asked the Ephesians and Philippians, the Colossians and the Romans, to pray for him; but from the others he would have received little benefit, for they were very weak in the faith, and troubled with sad disorders. He was in his imprisonment clear of those fickle and quarrelsome folk who had often pained him. His confinement under guard would not permit of his preaching himself to death, or wearing himself out with watchings: the soldier who kept him would make him reasonable; and so, I have no doubt, by the will of God he received precisely what he had asked his friends to pray for: "that I may come unto you with joy by the will of God, and may with you be refreshed." It would not have been Paul's will to have come to Rome with a chain on his wrists, binding him to a soldier; but he did so come, for this was the will of God, and was the surest way to his being refreshed. Paul refreshed the Romans and they refreshed him; and thus he had a happy sojourn in Rome. God was with him, and he had the privilege of testifying of Christ before the Roman emperor, and making Jesus to be known even in Cæsar's household. Thus, brethren, the Lord heard the prayer of his servants. He will also hear our prayers; not in my way, not in your way, but in the way which Paul has indicated, namely, "by the will of God." Therefore pray for a blessing, and leave the way of its coming to the good Lord who knoweth all things. Rest you sure that it will come by the will of God, and then it will be according to our will if we are in full accord with the Lord, as we ought to be. See the efficacy of prayer, then, in Paul's case; though the desire did not seem to be accomplished, yet it was so. When the Lord does not appear to hear his people's prayers he is hearing them none the less, yea, rather he is answering them all the more fully and graciously. When the Lord replies by terrible things in righteousness rather than by sweet, smooth deeds of kindness, he is doubly blessing us. Do not vessels often sail more swiftly with a side wind than they would do with a directly fair wind? The sails are more under the action of a side wind than if it blew directly behind them. The Lord often gives his people side gales, and these turn out to be the best they can have. Let us trust the divine wisdom, and rest assured that the Lord will do better things for us than we can ask or even think.

II. I have but little time left to notice THE BLESSING GIVEN, indeed it occupies but one verse in the text, and that verse is the shortest of the four, and therefore I may give it due consideration in a brief space. See how Paul, with all his anxiety to gain the prayers of his friends, cannot finish the chapter without uttering a benediction upon them. "Now the God of peace." What a blessed name! In the Old Testament Scriptures he is the "Lord of Hosts"; but that is never the style in the New Testament. The "Lord of Hosts" is God as he was revealed under the old dispensation: in the majesty of his power, "the Lord is a man of war, the Lord is his name." But now that our Lord Jesus Christ has further unveiled the Father, we see him as "the God of peace." Is not this a greater, sweeter, and more cheering title? O God of peace, we long for thy presence with us all!

What does Paul wish for them? "The God of peace be with you," not only "peace be with you," but, better far— "The God of peace," and so the source and fountain of peace. He wishes them, not the drops, but the fountain itself, not the light only, but the sun. He would have God himself to be with us as "the God of peace." He would have the Lord to fill us with an inward peace, so that we may never be disturbed in our minds. He would have the Lord shed abroad his own peace in our hearts, so that we may always feel at peace with God: no cloud coming between our souls and our heavenly Father: no ground of quarrel arising between us and the great King.

When "the God of peace" makes peace with himself, and so keeps our minds at peace within, he also creates peace with one another, so that we bear one another's burdens; and those who are strong are willing to bear the infirmities of the weak. "The God of peace be with you."

Our apostle says, "the God of peace be with you all,"—
not with some of you, with Priscilla and Aquila, but with
Mary, and Amplias, and Apelles, and Tryphena and
Tryphosa, and with "the beloved Persis, which laboured
much in the Lord," and with "Rufus chosen in the Lord,
and his mother," and "Philologus, and Julia, Nereus and
his sister, and Olympas, and all the saints which are with
them." The benediction is, "The God of peace be with you
all." Unless all are at peace, none can be perfectly quiet.
One brother who is quarrelsome can keep a whole church
in trouble. One fellow knocking about the boat may stop
the oarsmen, rend the sails, and run the boat on a rock. I
should not like one stray shot from a rifle to be travelling
near my windows; for even it all the other shots which are
in the armoury should lie quiet, that one flying danger
might be the end of me. Oh that the peace of God may be
with all the saints in all the churches! It is a blessed
benediction. Such a benediction we pronounce with all our
heart this morning—"Now the God of peace be with you
all. Amen."

Do you not think that Paul implies that this will be the
result of their prayer? If you will but strive together with
me in your prayers, then the God of peace will be with
you. May we not view it as the reward of such prayer? You
have prayed for the Lord's servant, and now God will bless
you with an abundance of peace. Or did he hint that this is
a necessary condition and cause of true prayer? When they
were all at peace among themselves, and happy in their
own minds, and full of communion with God, then they
would begin to pray for God's servants. Put it first or last,
may this peace come to you, and may there be hearty

pleading prayer to God that his blessing may rest upon the church, and upon the testimony of his servants.

Now we draw to a close, brethren. Prayer is sought most earnestly by me at this moment. I speak, I think, in the name of all those who have to stand prominent as preachers of the gospel of Christ. We beseech you, our beloved friends and fellow-labourers, that you wrestle together with us with God on our behalf, that our testimony may be with power and with success; for the times are very difficult. The very air is full of unbelief. The solid earth seems well nigh to tremble with unrest, social and political—a deep and terrible unrest that fills us with dark forebodings of the future. The hope of the world lies, under God, in the church of Jesus Christ. Therefore we beseech you, brethren, if in other days and softer times you did in a measure restrain prayer, do so no longer, but wrestle for us with God. What is coming no man knoweth. We wish not to play the Cassandra, prophesying evil things continually; but who is there, though he be a prophet bright-eyed as Isaiah, who can give you a good forecast? Are not all the signs of the times big with terror? Therefore to your tents, O Israel, and in your tents cry to God that a blessing may come upon this nation and the world.

Men are perishing all around us. Whatever may have been the state of the world in Paul's day—and it was, no doubt, horrible to the last degree—it is not much better now; and the population of the world has so largely increased since those days that all her problems have become more difficult. We are much better aware of the miseries of vast populations than people could have been in apostolic times. Paul knew but little of the world except that portion of it which bordered on the Mediterranean Sea: the whole world then seemed to lie in a nutshell; but now our discoverers and geographers, our steam-boats and telegraphs, have brought a greater world close to our doors. We share with the sorrows of India; we groan in the darkness of Africa; the cries of China are at our doors, and Egypt's griefs are our own. If a population anywhere is starving or suffering oppression our newspapers declare the evil to all readers, and general feeling is awakened. Our sympathies for humanity are called forth much more than in former times; and, so far, this is good; but then it heaps heavier burdens upon the thoughtful, and increases the terrible responsibility of those who are able to lend a helping hand. Increase of knowledge demands increase of prayer. "The world for Jesus" is our motto; but how the world for Jesus if the church of Jesus does not wrestle in her prayers?

Dear brethren, do remember that the truth alone, if not enforced by the Spirit of God, will not sink into the hearts of men. They say, "Truth is mighty, and will prevail"; but this is only half the case. If you put truth upon a shelf, and let the dust lie on her record, of what use will it be to men? Truth unknown, how can it enlighten? Truth not felt, how can it renew? There must therefore be the preacher to call attention to truth; but how shall they preach except they be sent? and how shall they be sent aright except in the power of the Holy Ghost? and how can we expect the Holy Ghost if we do not ask for his working? Wherefore, we pray you, wrestle together with us in your prayers, that the Holy Ghost may go forth with the truth and by the truth.

This will be to your profit. No man hears his pastor preach without deriving some benefit from him, if he has earnestly prayed for him. The best hearers, who get the most out of a man, are those who love him best, and pray most for him. God can make us dry wells to you if you offer no prayers for us. He can make us clouds that are full of rain, if you have pleaded with God on our behalf.

But the master argument with which we close is that which Paul mentions—"for Christ's sake." Oh, for God's sake, for his name and glory's sake, if you would honour the Father, if you would let Jesus see of the travail of his soul, wrestle together with us in your prayers for the divine working. It is so, brother, you know it is so, we are wholly dependent upon the Spirit of God. If it be so, that without God's blessing we can do nothing, and that God's blessing is given if we inquire of God for it, then I need not press you further—you will pray for me and for other preachers of the word. If your hearts are right, you will each one resolve to offer special, continuous, and fervent prayer in private, and in your families and in our holy convocations, and these shall deepen into an agony before God, and then a blessing shall be given us which we shall scarcely have room enough to receive. Lord, teach us to pray!

7

THE LOVE OF GOD AND THE
PATIENCE OF CHRIST (1888)

*"And the Lord direct your hearts into the love of God, and into the
patient waiting for Christ."—2 Thessalonians 3:5.*

*"Oh, that the Lord would direct you into the antiquity of his love. It
shall make you greatly prize that love to think that it had no
beginning, and shall never, never have an end."*

—

FOR the moment, Paul in spirit is coasting the purple
shores of the celestial country. With his Thessalonian
friends he is making a joyful voyage within hail of
Immanuel's land. The sail is bright with the sunlight, and
the keel is marking a silver track behind it. The apostle's
happy soul has left far in the stern the deceivableness of
unrighteousness and the rocks of error. It comes into his
heart that he would gladly steer his friends into certain of
those lovely creeks which run up far into the inner recesses
of the sacred fatherland. Shall he turn the helm that way?

144

He pauses; for the navigation is difficult. One must be greatly expert to thread the streams which descend from the sunny fountains. It is not given even to all saints to follow safely all the windings of the rivers of delight. Paul had been with his brethren at sea in the place where the Lord sank all their transgressions in the depths, and he had been with them in sore affliction when neither sun nor moon appeared, and in all such seafaring he was in his element; but, brave pilot as he was, he could not pretend to penetrate all the richer and rarer experiences which bring elect souls nearest to the heart of the great Father; and therefore, instead of offering to be their pilot, he bowed his head, and prayed, "The Lord direct your hearts into the love of God, and into the patient waiting for Christ."

The special entrance into the goodly land, which the apostle desired for his friends, was one which mere insight, wit, knowledge, or instruction could never give them. If so, he would have directed their minds that way at once. But the perception of the heavenlies is only given to heavenly faculties. The attainments which Paul desired for his friends were not beliefs of the head, but indwellings of the heart. To return to our figure of sailing up the creeks and rivers into the centre of the glorious country—that delicious voyage was only possible to the more refined and spiritual powers of the soul. Those sweet waters could only be navigated by the heart, and the heart itself would need divine direction before it could find the entrance to them. There is a path which the vulture's eye has not seen, and the lion's whelp hath not trodden: only God seeth and knoweth it. The Beulah country of spiritual wisdom, especially in its higher reaches, is a matter for personal revelation from God to each one of his own. We are here hopelessly in the dark if we have no light from above; and even with that light we do but see the difficult nature of our way, and fail to enter upon it, until the light becomes a force, and he whom we desire to know directs our hearts into communion with himself. Yes, yonder are the radiant coasts, and the rivers of life up which our barque might sail into the centre of "the island of the innocent"; yet our great apostle does not rush into the office of pilot, but humbly acts as intercessor, crying, "The Lord direct your hearts into the love of God."

All this whets our desires! Who would not wish to go where only choice spirits can enter, and where these can only come as the Lord directs their hearts?

Paul could give his converts external directions, he could guide his more advanced brethren in the work, walk, and warfare of life; and he did so with all simplicity and earnestness. He urged them to abound in this grace, and to avoid that folly; but he felt that his exhortation would be inefficient unless their hearts were touched. Here he felt his own powerlessness, and so he cast the grand matter of heart-work upon the Lord himself. As the heart naturally baffles all physicians, so spiritually it is far beyond our knowledge. Who among ministers can guide you? Therefore may "the Lord direct your hearts."

God alone knows the heart, and God alone can rule it: for this ruling Paul makes request. "The Lord direct your hearts." Let us borrow his prayer, and turn it to our own personal use: "Domine dirige nos."

The place for God in reference to the heart is that of supreme director. When the Lord lays his hand on the heart, which is the helm of the ship, then the whole vessel is rightly directed: this, therefore, is what we beseech him to do. When the Holy Spirit comes into the heart, and takes supreme control of the affections, then the whole life and conversation are after a godly sort. Oh, that he may prove this fact to each one of us! Some think much of liberty: I long far more to be in perfect subjection to the Lord my God. Oh, how I wish for a Master, a Dictator, a Director! Oh, that my Lord would take the reins, and bring my every thought into captivity to his own will, henceforth and for ever!

What a heavenly content I feel in yielding myself to the sacred Trinity! The God who made us may most fitly be called upon to govern us. When we recognize the glory of the whole Godhead, we perceive the perfect suitability of such direction as will come from the Three-One God. Albeit that the Holy Spirit is not mentioned in this verse by name, yet he is mentioned by his operations, for it is the Spirit of God that deals with the hearts of believers. I take rare pleasure in our text, because we have the blessed Trinity in unity in these few words, "The Lord"—that is, the Holy Spirit who dwells within believers—"direct your hearts into the love of God (by whom I understand the Father), and into the patient waiting for Christ." May the Trinity in Unity work with us, and fulfil in each of us this prayer of the apostle, that our hearts may be directed into the love of God, and into the patient waiting for Christ!

Paul would have his Thessalonian friends advance in a straight line. Our heart is to be as a vessel that is not left to beat about, nor to come into harbour by a circuitous route; but is steered directly into the fair haven. May the Spirit of God take us and give us a straight tendency towards the holiest things, and then at once bring us into the love of God, and into the patient waiting for Christ.

But here we must do a little translating or interpreting. Observe in the Revised Version a difference of translation. There we read "into the patience of Christ." This is a great improvement upon our former translation; but, although it is accurate, it is not complete: it does not take up the whole of the meaning. In our Authorized Version we have "the patient waiting for Christ," but in its margin we find "into the patience of Christ"; showing that the earlier translators felt that "the patience of Christ" would be a good translation; and yet, after considering it in all its bearings, they thought that Paul did not quite mean the patience of Christ, but that he meant a patience which we exert towards Christ. Is there not weight in this? Does not the context support it? As the love into which we are to be directed is love to God, so the patience into which we are to be directed must be a patience towards Christ. Our grand old translators expressed this truth by language which may be inaccurate as mere wording, but it is deeply correct as to its sense. Surely Paul did mean "the patience towards Christ which manifests itself in the patient waiting for Christ." If you consider all this, you will see that we have no infant-class lesson in the text before us! Here are nuts for young men who have cut their wisdom-teeth. May the good Spirit help us to reach the kernels.

Having turned the text over many times, I thought that we might be able to gather up a considerable amount of its real meaning if we thought of it thus: first, here are two precious things for us to enter into—the love of God and the patience of Christ; and, secondly, here are two eminent virtues to be acquired by us: the love of God, that is, love to God, and the patience of Christ—the patient waiting for Christ.

I. To begin, then, here are TWO PRECIOUS THINGS FOR US TO ENTER INTO. We cannot enter into them except as the Lord directs our hearts. There is a straight entrance into them, but we do not readily find it. It needs the Holy Spirit to direct our feet along the narrow way which leads to this great blessedness.

The first precious thing which we are to enter is the love of God. Beloved, we know the love of God in various ways. Many know it by having heard of it, even as a blind man may thus know the charms of an Alpine landscape. Poor knowledge this! Others of us have tasted of the love of God, have talked about the love of God, have prayed, and have sung concerning the love of God. All very well, but Paul meant a dove of a brighter feather. To be directed into the love of God is quite another thing from all that we can be told of it. A fair garden is before us. We look over the wall, and are even allowed to stand at the door, while one handeth out to us baskets of golden apples. This is very delightful. Who would not be glad to come so near as this to the garden of heavenly delights? Yet it is something more to be shown the door, to have the latch lifted, to see the gateway opened, and to be gently directed into the Paradise of God. This is what is wanted—that we may be directed into the love of God. Oh, that we may feel something of it while we meditate upon it!

Beloved, we come, when we are taught of the Spirit of God, to enter into the love of God by seeing its central importance. We see that the love of God is the source and centre, fountain and foundation of all our salvation, and of all else that we receive from God. At the first we are much taken up with pardoning grace. We are largely engrossed with those royal robes of righteousness with which our nakedness is covered. We are delighted with the viands of the marriage banquet: we eat the fat and we drink the sweet. What else would you expect from starving souls admitted to the abundant supplies of heavenly grace? Afterwards we begin more distinctly to think of the love that spread the feast, the love that provided the raiment, the love that invited us to the banquet, and gently led us to take our place in it. This does not always come at first; but I pray that none of us may be long receiving the gifts of love without kissing the hand of love; that none of us may be content to have had much forgiven without coming and washing the feet of our forgiving Lord with our tears, and declaring our deep and true love to him. O saved soul, may the Lord fill thee with personal love to that personal Saviour, through whom all blessings come to thee! Remember, thou hast all good things because God loveth thee! Remember that every cake of the heavenly manna, every cup of the living water, comes to thee because of his great love wherewith he loved thee. This will put a sweetness into what thou receivest even greater than that which is there intrinsically, sweet though God's mercies be in their own nature and quality. Oh, to enter into God's love by perceiving it to be the well-head of every stream of mercy by which we are refreshed!

If we further enter into the love of God, we see its immeasurable greatness. There is a little word which you have often heard, which I beg to bring before you again— that little word "so." "God so loved the world that he gave his only begotten Son, that whosoever believeth in him should not perish, but have everlasting life." Come, ye surveyors, bring your chains, and try to make a survey of this word "so." Nay, that is not enough. Come hither, ye that make our national surveys, and lay down charts for all nations. Come, ye who map the sea and land, and make a chart of this word "so." Nay, I must go further. Come hither, ye astronomers, that with your optic glasses spy out spaces before which imagination staggers, come hither and encounter calculations worthy of all your powers! When you have measured between the horns of space, here is a task that will defy you—"God so loved the world." If you enter into that, you will know that all this love is to you— that while Jehovah loves the world, yet he loves you as much as if there were nobody else in all the world to love. God can pour the infinite love of his heart upon one object, and yet, for all that, can love ten thousand times ten thousand of his creatures just as much. O heir of God, thy store of love is not diminished because the innumerable company of thy brethren share it with thee! Thy Father loves each child as well as if he had no other. Peer into this abyss of love. Plunge into this sea. Dive into this depth unsearchable. Oh, that God might direct you into the immeasurable greatness of this love!

Neither be thou afraid to enter into this love by remembering its antiquity. Some fight shy of the great truth of the eternal electing love of God; but to me it is as wafers made with honey. What music lies in that sentence—"Yea, I have loved thee with an everlasting love"! When this great world, the sun, and moon, and stars, had not yet flashed the morning of their little day, the Lord Jehovah loved his people with an everlasting love. In the divine purposes, which were not of yesterday, nor even of that date of which Scripture speaks as "In the beginning," when the Lord created the heavens and the earth, God loved his own people. He had chosen you, thought of you, provided for you, and made ten thousand forecasts of lovingkindness towards you, or ever the earth was. Beloved believer, you were graven on the hands of Christ even then. Oh, that the Lord would direct you into the antiquity of his love. It shall make you greatly prize that love to think that it had no beginning, and shall never, never have an end.

Again, I pray that we may be directed into the love of God as to its infallible constancy. The unchangeable Jehovah never ceases to love his people. It would be a wretched business to be directed into the love of God only to find it a thing of the past. O believing soul, thou hast not to deal with things which once were gems of the mine, but now are dreams of the night. Oh, no! the love of God abides for ever the same. When thou art in darkness the Lord still sees thee with an eye of love.

"He saw thee ruined in the fall,
Yet loved thee notwithstanding all."

When thou wast without strength, "in due time Christ died for the ungodly." Since thou hast known him he has never varied in his love. When thou hast grown cold he has loved thee; when thou hast grown cruel he has loved thee. Thou hast grievously provoked him till he has taken down his rod, and made thee smart; but he has loved thee in the smiting. With God there is as much love in chastening as in caressing. He never abates in fervour towards his ancient friends. Has he not said, "I am the Lord; I change not; therefore ye sons of Jacob are not consumed"? I pray the Lord to direct us into the immutability of his divine love, for this is a great holdfast in the day of soul-trouble. When conscious of imperfection, when darkened by the shadow of a great fault, when trembling under apprehension of wrath, it draws you back again if you can feel, "Still my Father is my Father, still will he receive his wandering child, and press his prodigal to his bosom, and rejoice over me, and say, 'This my son was dead, and is alive again.' " O child of God, thy questionings of divine love are grievous to thy God; but if thou canst learn this truth and be led into it—that he loves thee evermore the same—it will help thee right graciously.

This love we ought to know, and if the Lord will lead us into it we shall know, that it is omnipresent. I mean by this, that whatever condition we may be in, the Lord is still active in love towards us. Thou art going across the sea to a far country, but thy Father's love will be as near thee on the blue wave as on the greensward of Old England. Thou hast come out to-night alone: time was when thou didst come to the house of God in company; but it may be that graves and desertions furnish sad reasons for thy present solitude. Still, thou art not alone, thy Father's love is with thee. Thou art tonight, perhaps, in a very strange part of thy spiritual experience: thou hast not gone this way heretofore. But the road is not new to eternal love. Go where thou mayest, the air is still about thee: go where thou mayest, thy Father's love is all around thee. Higher than thy soarings, deeper than thy sinkings, is all-surrounding love. Thou art going home, perhaps to a bed, from which thou shalt not rise for months. Thou hast no apprehension just now of what lies before thee in the immediate future. It is as well thou shouldst not know. I should be slow to lift the curtain of merciful concealment even if it were in my power to do so. There is no necessity to know details when one or two grand facts provide for all contingencies. Trouble not thyself about the morrow. If thou art to be sick, or if thou art to die, thy Father's love will be with thee still. Therefore go on, and fear not. He cannot, will not, turn away from thee. An omnipresent God means omnipresent love, and omnipotence goes hand-in-hand with omnipresence. The Lord will show himself strong on the behalf of them that trust him. His love, which never fails, is attended by a power that fainteth not, neither is weary. Oh, may the Lord lead you into such love as this! May the Holy Ghost lead you into the innermost secret of this joy of joys, this bliss unspeakable!

And I would also wish that you may be directed into the love of God as to its entire agreement with his justice, his holiness, his spotless purity. I firmly believe that God loves sinners, but I am equally sure that he hates sin. I do believe that he delights in mercy, but I am equally clear that he never dishonours his justice, nor frustrates the sternest threatening of his law. It is our joy that a holy God loves us, and does not find it needful to stain his holiness to save the unclean. We are loved by one so just, so righteous, that he could not pardon us without atonement. Even to-day he will never spare our sins, but he will drive the love of them out of us by chastisement, even as he has washed the guilt of them away by the precious blood of his dear Son. O beloved, we have a holy God, who is determined to make us holy. He would have us love our wives; and he sets before us a holy model—"Even as Christ also loved the church, and gave himself for it; that he might sanctify and cleanse it with the washing of water by the Word." All true love goes towards purification; and the true love of God goes that way with an invincible current, that can never be turned aside. O believer, thy God loves thee so well that he will not let a darling sin stay in thy heart; he loves thee so strongly that he will not spare any iniquity in thee. "You only have I known of all the families of the earth; therefore I will punish you for your iniquities." Out of his pure love he will chasten and refine till he has made us pure and able to abide in fellowship with his perfect nature.

I have thus spoken a little upon a vast theme. I fear it will seem to you mere surface-work; and yet I pray that it may lead you to deep knowledge of divine things, so that you may apprehend God's love as yours, and then may feel the power, the unction, the savour, which come out of his love, making all your heart as sweet and aromatic as a chamber in which a box of precious ointment has been broken. Oh, that you might be led into the innermost secret of the Lord's love till it shall saturate you, influence you, take possession of you, carry you right away! The Lord direct you into the love of God.

The second part of the prayer upon which we shall have to dwell is, "The Lord direct your hearts into the patience of Christ." Now, beloved, I have another great sea before me, and who am I that I should act as your convoy over this main ocean? Here I am lost. I cannot take my bearings. I am a lone speck upon the infinite. I will imitate the wise apostle, and pray, "The Lord direct your hearts into the patience of Christ."

What a patience that was which Jesus exhibited for us in our redemption! To come from heaven to earth, to dwell in poverty and neglect, and find no room even in the inn! Admire the patience of Bethlehem. To hold his tongue for thirty years—who shall estimate the wonderful patience of Nazareth and the carpenter's shop! When he spoke, to be despised and rejected of men, what patience for him whom Cherubim obey! Oh, the patience of the Christ to be tempted of the devil! One can hardly tell what patience Christ must have had to let the devil come within ten thousand miles of him, for he was able to keep him far down in the abyss below his feet. There is not much in a patience which cannot help itself; but you well know that all the while Christ could have conquered all foes, chased away all suffering, and kept off all temptation; but for our sakes, as Captain of our salvation, that he might be made perfect through suffering, his patience had its perfect work, right on to Gethsemane. Do you need that I tell you this? Golgotha, with all its woes, its "lama sabachthani," its abysmal griefs, do I need remind you of the patience of Christ for us when the Lord laid on him the iniquity of us all? Patient as a lamb, he opened not his mouth, but stood in omnipotence of patience, all-sufficient to endure. Ye have heard of the patience of Job, but ye have need to enter into the patience of Jesus.

Oh, the patience within Christ himself! God never seems so like a God as when he divinely rules himself. I can understand his shaking earth and heaven with his word; but that he should possess his own soul in patience is far more incomprehensible. Marvel that omnipotent love should restrain omnipotence itself. In the life and death of our Lord Jesus we see almighty patience. He was very sensitive—very sensitive of sin, very sensitive of unkindness, and yet with all that sensitiveness he showed no petulance, but bore himself in all the calm grandeur of Godhead. He was not quick to resent an ill, but he was patient to the uttermost. As I have said before, there went with his sensitiveness the power at any time to avenge himself and deliver himself, but he would not use it. Legions of angels would have been glad to come to his rescue, but he bowed alone in the garden, and gave himself up to the betrayer without a word. And all the while was most tender and graciously considerate of everybody but himself. He spoke burning words sometimes: his mouth could be like the red lips of a volcano as he poured out the burning lava of denunciation upon "scribes and Pharisees, hypocrites"; but the resentment was never aroused by any injury done to himself. When he looked that way it was always gentleness: he cried, "Father, forgive them; for they know not what they do." Oh, the wondrous patience of heaven's own Christ!

Enter into his patience with us as well as for us. How he put up with each one of us when we would not come to him! How he wept over us when we neglected him! How he drew us with constancy of love when we tugged against the cords! And when we came to him, and since we have been with him, what patience he has had with our ill-manners! If I had been Christ, I would have discharged such a servant as I have been long ago. Often have I gone to his feet, and cried,

"Dismiss me not thy service, Lord."

I knew how justly he might have stripped his livery from my back; but he has not done so. Have you not often wondered that he should still love you? He is affianced to you, and he hateth putting away; but is it not marvellous that he keeps his troth with you, and will do so, though you have often defiled yourself, and forgotten him? Blessed fact, the ring is on his finger rather than on yours, and the marriage is as sure as his love. He will present you unto himself, "without spot, or wrinkle, or any such thing," one of these days. But oh! his patience with each one of us. How he has put up with our unbelief, our mistrust, our hard hearts, our indifference, our strange ways! Never lover so kind as he! On our part never return so unworthy. Blessed be the patience of our Best Beloved!

Now, beloved, what is wanted is that we be directed into this patience of Christ. The choicest saints in different ages of the world have studied most the passion of our Lord; and although nowadays we hear from the wise men that it is sensuous to talk about the cross and the five wounds, and so forth, for my part I feel that no contemplation ever does me so much real benefit as that which brings me very near my bleeding Lord. The cross for me! The cross for me! Here is doctrine humbling, softening, melting, elevating, sanctifying. Here is truth that is of heaven, and yet comes down to earth: love that lifts me away from earth even to the seventh heaven. Have you ever read the words of holy Bernard, when his soul was all on fire with love of that dear name of which he so sweetly sang,

> "Jesus the very thought of thee
> With sweetness fills my breast."

Why, Bernard is poet, philosopher, and divine, and yet a child in love. Have you studied Rutherford's letters and the wondrous things which he says about his own dear Lord? For an hour at glory's gate commend me to heavenly Master Rutherford. Have you never held fellowship with George Herbert, that saintly songster? Hear him as he cries,

> "How sweetly doth my Master sound! My Master!
>   As ambergris leaves a rich scent
>   Unto the taster,
>   So do these words a sweet content,

An oriental fragrancy, My Master!"

O friends, I can wish you no greater blessing than to be directed into these two things—the love of God, and the patience of your Saviour. Enter both at the same time. You cannot divide them; why should you? The love of God shines best in the patience of the Saviour; and what is the patience of Christ but the love of the Father? "What God hath joined together, let no man put asunder." May the Lord lead us into both of them at this hour, and continue upon us the heavenly process all the rest of our lives, in all experiences of sorrow and of rapture, and in all moods and growths of our spirit!

II. But now I must ask your attention for the few minutes that remain to me to what is, perhaps, still the real gist of the text: HERE ARE TWO EMINENT VIRTUES TO BE ACQUIRED.

"The Lord direct your hearts into the love of God." Beloved, let the love of God to you flow into your hearts, and abide there till it settles down, and bears on its surface the cream of love to God, yielded by your own heart. The only way to love God is to let God's love to you dwell in your soul till it transforms your soul into itself. Love to God grows out of the love of God.

Well, now, concerning love to God: if you receive it fully into your souls it will nourish the contemplative life. You will want to be alone. You will prefer to sit silently at Jesus' feet, while others wrangle over the little politics of the house. You will give up being busy-bodies, talking in six peoples' houses in an hour: quietude will charm you. You will love no company so much as the society of him who is the Best and the Most. To be with God in quiet will be your highest enjoyment. You will not say, as some do, "I must have recreation." Contemplation of God is recreation to the child of God. It creates the soul anew; and is not this the truest re-creation? Whenever God's creation in us seems to have grown a little dim, love to God will gender and nourish the contemplative life, and so make us come forth as new creatures, fresh from our Maker's holy hand.

It will also animate the active life if you love God. You will feel that you must yield fruit unto your Lord. Your soul, when full of the love of God, will cry, "I must go after the wanderer; I must care for the poor; I must teach the ignorant." You cannot love God and be lazy. Love to God will stir you up. Contemplation teaches you to sit still, and this is no trifling lesson; but after sitting still, you rise with greater energy to go about the one thing needful, namely, the service of your Lord's love.

Love to God will also arouse enthusiasm. We want more persons in the church who will be a little daring—rash men and women who will do things which nobody else would think of doing, such as will make their prudent friends hold up their hands and say, "How could you? If you had consulted with me, I could have given you many a wise hint as to how it ought to have been done." This has been my lot of late. I have been surfeited with notions as to how I should have acted. Yes, my friend, I know you of old. You have wisdom at your fingers' ends. But let me quietly whisper that you would have done nothing at all;

you would have been too anxious to save yourself from trouble. It is an easy thing to tell a man how he ought to have done it; and yet that man perhaps may be suffering intensely for having done bravely a well-meant deed. Instead of your showing sympathy with him, you treat him to the remark, "It might have been done better in another way." There was never a child that was near drowning but what the man that plunged in and drew him out of the river ought to have done it in a better way. He wetted himself too much; he waited too long; or he handled the drowning one too roughly. Alas, for silly criticisms of gracious deeds! If you come to love God with all consuming zeal, you will not be hindered by criticisms. You will testify for Jesus freely, because you cannot help yourself. It has to be done: somebody has to sacrifice himself to do it, and you say to yourself, "Here am I, Lord; send me. At every risk or hazard, send me. For thy dear love's sake I count it joy to suffer shame or loss. I count it life to suffer death that I may honour thee." Love to God will arouse enthusiasm.

It will also stimulate holy desire. They that love God can never have enough of him—certainly never too much. Sometimes they are found pining after him. When we love the Lord, we chide the laggard hours which keep us from his coming. Time has not wings enough.

> "My heart is with him on his throne,
>   And ill can brook delay,
> Each moment listening for the voice,
>   'Rise up, and come away.' "

A heavenly love-sickness sometimes makes God's handmaids swoon; for they long to see the Beloved face to face, and to be like him, and to be with him where he is. The Lord direct your hearts into the love of God in some such fashion as this; for it will make you sit loose by all things here below. Do you never feel that your wings are growing? Do you never sigh, "Oh, that I had wings like a dove! for then would I fly away, and be at rest"?

And this love, better still, will transform the character. It is wonderful what a difference love makes in the person that is possessed with it. A poor timid hen that will fly away from every passer-by, loves its offspring, and when it has its chicks about it, it will fight like a very griffin for its young. And when the love of Christ comes into a timid believer, how it changes him! It takes the love of sin away, and implants a sublime nature. God only knows what a mortal man can yet become. Of women sunken in sin, what saints the Lord has made when he has filled them with his love! When the sun shines on a bit of glass bottle far away, it flashes like a diamond. A little fleecy vapour in the sky rivals an angel's wing when the sun pours itself upon it. Our Lord can put so much of himself, by means of his love, into the hearts of his people, that they may be mistaken for himself. John made a blunder in heaven, and fell at the feet of one of his brethren the prophets; for he had come to be so much like his Lord, that John could hardly tell the one from the other. Had he forgotten that word, "We shall be like him; for we shall see him as he is"? It doth not yet appear what we shall be, but love is the transfiguring power in the hand of the Holy Spirit. If the heart be directed into the love of Christ, it is on the highway to holiness.

Lastly—I am sorry that time will fly so fast just now—we want our hearts to be directed into patience towards Christ. What a subject is this! Beloved, if our heart is directed into patience towards Christ, we shall suffer in patience for our Lord's sake, and we shall not complain. Those about us will say, "It is wonderful how resigned he seems"; or, "How gladly she bears grief for love of Christ!" And if it be the suffering of reproach and scorn for Jesus' sake, if we are directed into the patience of Christ, it will not seem to be any trouble at all. We shall bear it calmly, and in our hearts we shall laugh at those who laugh at us for Jesus' sake.

Yet it is not all patience of suffering that we want. We want the patience of forbearing. We must learn not to answer those who blaspheme. "Bear, and forbear, and silent be." Chew the cud in peace. Put up with much. When reviled, revile not again. The Lord direct your hearts into the patience of Christ.

We shall also want the patience of working—working on when nothing comes of it—pleading on with souls that are not converted—preaching when preaching seems to have no effect—teaching when the children do not care to learn. We need the patience of Christ, who set his face like a flint, and would accomplish his work cost what it may. He never turned aside from it for a moment. The Lord direct our hearts into patient working.

Then there is the patience of watching in prayer—not giving it up because you have not received an answer. What? Did a friend say she had prayed for seventeen years for a certain mercy, and now meant to ask it no more? Sister, make it eighteen years, and when you have got to the end of eighteen make it nineteen. May the Lord direct our hearts into the patience of Christ in prayer! We long kept him waiting: we need not complain if he makes us tarry his leisure. Still believe; still hope; still wrestle, until the break of day.

Pray for the patience of waiting his will, saying, "Let him do what seemeth him good." Though it be for months, for years, wait on. Christ is glorified by our patience. Depend on it, the best way in which certain of us can extol him is by letting him have his way with us. Even though he plunge me into seven boiling caldrons one after the other, I will say: Let him do what he wills with his own, and I am his own. I am sure that he does not make the furnace one degree too hot. If he means to give his servant ten troubles, let his heavy hand fall even to the tenth, if so he pleases.

We want to be directed into patience towards Christ, and especially in patience in waiting for his coming. That, no doubt, is very justly inferred, and so it is put in our translation very prominently: "Patient waiting for Christ." He will come, brothers; he will come, sisters. It is true the interpreters of the Book of Revelation told us that he was to come three hundred years ago, and there are thousands upon thousands of books in the British Museum which were very dogmatic upon this point, and yet they have all been disproved by the lapse of time. Men were as sure as sure could be that Christ would come just then; and he did not, for he was bound by his Word, but not by their interpretation of it. He will come at the appointed hour. To the jots and tittles God's word will stand. He will come to the tick of the clock. We know not when; we need not ask; but let us wait.

Just now some of you may be, as I am, troubled because the Lord does not yet appear to vindicate his cause; and there is noise and triumph among the priests of Baal. The Lord direct our hearts into the patience of Christ. It is all right. Clouds gather; the darkness becomes more dense. The thunder rolls; friends flee in confusion. What next? Well, perhaps, before we have hardly time for dread, silver drops of gracious rain may fall, and the sun may break through the clouds, and we may say to ourselves, "Who would have thought it?"

> "Ye fearful saints, fresh courage take,
>   The clouds ye so much dread
> Are big with mercy, and shall break
>   In blessings on your head."

May the Lord direct each one of us into the patient waiting for Christ!

I am sorry, very sorry, that there are persons here to whom all this must seem a strange lot of talk. They know nothing about it. Dear souls, you cannot at present know anything about it. You must first be born again. A total change of heart must come over you before you can enter into the love of God or the patience of Christ. May that change take place to-night, before you go to sleep! If the Lord shall lead you to seek his face, this is the way to seek it: trust his dear Son. Lifted on the cross is Jesus Christ, the great Propitiation for sin. Look to him, and looking alone to him, you shall be saved. He will give you the new heart and the right spirit with which you shall be enabled to enter into the love of God and the patience of Christ. The Lord direct you at this very hour, for Jesus' sake! Amen.

8
DIVINE LOVE AND ITS GIFTS (1873)

*"Now our Lord Jesus Christ himself, and God, even our Father,
which hath loved us, and hath given us everlasting consolation and
good hope through grace, comfort your hearts, and stablish you in
every good word and work."—2 Thessalonians 2:16, 17.*

*"It is, to my mind, quite understandable that the good and gracious
God should be merciful towards his creatures: but it is a far greater
thing that he should love them."*

—

THE Thessalonians had been much disturbed by the
predictions of divers persons that the day of Christ was at
hand. There always have been pretenders to prophetic
knowledge, who have fixed dates for the end of the world,
and by their fanaticism have driven many into lunatic
asylums and disturbed the peace of others; some of this
band had worried the saints at Thessalonica. The apostle,
after beseeching them not to be soon shaken in mind or
troubled by such follies, went on to beg them not to be

deceived by forged letters or pretended prophets, and then prayed for them that they might possess abiding consolation, which would keep them calmly persevering in holiness. His prayer is singularly emphatic; he cries to the Lord Jesus Christ himself, and to God, even our Father, to comfort their hearts, that by such consolations they may be so confirmed that nothing may cause them to decline from any holy enterprise or testimony. Perhaps, during their fright some of them had ceased from service, reckoning it vain to go on with anything when the world was so near its end; therefore, Paul would have them calmed in spirit that they might diligently persevere in their Christian course. That which frightens us from duty cannot be a good thing; true comfort stablishes us in every good word and work.

It is an ill wind which blows no one any good. We owe to the needless alarms of the Thessalonians this prayer, which, while it was useful for them, is also instructive for us; and I pray that while we look into it we may be led into deep thoughts of the love of God, and not into thoughts only, but into a personal enjoyment of that love, so that this morning the love of God may be shed abroad in our hearts by the Holy Spirit which is given unto us. To hear of the love of God is sweet—to believe it most precious—but to enjoy it is Paradise below the skies; may God grant us a taste thereof this morning.

I shall first call your earnest attention to the blessed fact recorded in our text, that "our Lord Jesus Christ himself, and God, even our Father, hath loved us;" then we will dwell upon the past manifestations of that love—"he hath given us everlasting consolation and good hope through grace:" and then we shall dwell for a while upon the prayer which Paul based upon this love and its manifestation, "that God would comfort your hearts, and stablish you in every good word and work."

I. First, then, dear brethren, let me ask your hearts, as well as your minds, to consider THIS GLORIOUS FACT: "Our Lord Jesus Christ himself, and God, even our Father, hath loved us." I cannot help repeating my frequent remark that the love of God is a theme fitter for the solitary contemplation of each person than for public utterance or explanation. It is to be felt, but it never can be uttered. Who can speak of love? In what language shall we sing its sweetness? No other word, nor set of words, can utter its meaning. You may go round about and make a long definition, but you have not defined it; and he who never felt his heart glow with it will remain an utter stranger to it, depict it as you may. Love must be felt in the heart, it cannot be learned from a dictionary. "God hath loved us." I want you not so much to follow what I shall have to say upon that wonderful fact, as to try and think over this thought for yourselves. God hath loved us. Drink into that truth. Take the word, lay it under your tongue, and let it dissolve like a wafer made with honey, till it sweetens all your soul.

God hath loved us? Let me remark that it does not say "He pitied us." That would be true, for "like as a father pitieth his children, so the Lord pitieth them that fear him." Pity is one degree below love and often leads to it, but it is not love: you may pity a person whom, apart from his sufferings, you would heartily dislike. You cannot endure the man, yet are you sorrowful that he should be so pained. Nor does the text declare that God has had mercy upon us. I could comprehend that, ay, and bless God for ever, because his mercy endureth for ever. It is, to my mind, quite understandable that the good and gracious God should be merciful towards his creatures: but it is a far greater thing that he should love them. Love is a feeling vastly more to be valued than mere mercy. Merciful is a man to his beast, but he does not love it; merciful has many a man been to his enemies, for whom he has had no degree of affection; but God doth not merely pity us and have mercy upon us, he loves us. Neither can this word be bartered for that of benevolence. There is an aspect under which God is love to all his creatures, because he is benevolent and wishes well towards all things that he hath made, but Paul was not thinking of that when he said, "God hath loved us, and given us everlasting consolation." A mother is not said to be benevolent towards her child, nor a husband coldly benevolent towards his bride: benevolence would be a poor, poor, substitute for love; love is as infinitely beyond benevolence as the gold of kings in value exceeds the stone of the quarry. We have frequently heard theologians declare that the love of God towards his elect is the love of complacency, and the statement, though perhaps true, is most frosty. One would not like to strike out the word "love," and put in its place the word "complacency." It would be like setting up a globe of ice in the place of the sun. Love glows with sunlight, complacency has at best but cold moonlike beams. No, we must hold to the words, "hath loved us." Truly, the Lord has a complacency in his people as he sees them in Christ, but he has much more than that. He is benevolent towards his people, and towards all creatures, but he is much more than that towards us; he is merciful, he is pitiful, he is everything that is good, but he is more than that—he "hath loved us." You know, mother, how you look upon that dear child of yours as you hold it in your arms. Why, it seems part of yourself. You love it as you love yourself, and your thoughts of it do not differ from your thoughts about your own welfare: the child is intertwisted with your being. Now God also hath united us to himself by cords of love and bonds of affection, and he thinks of us as he thinks of himself. I can express this, but I cannot explain it. Even now I feel much more inclined to sit down and weep for joy of heart that God could ever love me, than to try and speak to you. He made the heavens, and I am less than the veriest speck—yet he loves me. It is his eternal arm that has held up the universe in all ages, and I am as a leaf of the forest, green awhile, but soon to grow sere and to be buried with my fellows, yet the Eternal loves me, and always will love me. With his great infinite heart he loves me—as a God he loves me, divinely loves me. It is a conquering thought, it utterly overcomes us and crushes us with its weight of joy; it bows us to the ground and casts us into a swoon of ecstasy when it is realised by the mind. "God, even our Father, hath loved us."

Now, permit the other side of the thought to shine upon your minds, the marvel is not merely that God hath loved, but that he hath loved us, so insignificant, so frail, so foolish, let us add—for this increases the marvel—so sinful, and therefore so uncomely, so ungrateful, and therefore so provoking, so wilfully obstinate in returning to old sins again, and therefore so deserving to be abhorred and rejected! I can imagine the Lord's love to the apostles. We can sometimes think of his love to the early saints without any great wonder, and of his love to the patriarchs and to the confessors and the martyrs, and to some eminently holy men whose biographies have charmed us: but that our Lord Jesus Christ, himself God, even our Father, should have loved us, is a world of wonders! And if I put it into the singular number, and say, "Who loved me and gave himself for me," it shall ever stand first of all miracles to my soul's apprehension that I should be the object of divine affection. Dear brethren and sisters, I leave this meditation with you, I cannot speak of it, I beseech you to baptise your souls into it, and to let this one thought overwhelm you this day,—"God, even our Father, hath loved us."

Let me carry your minds onward a little further. Remember that the eternal love of God is the great fountain and source from which proceed all the spiritual blessings which we enjoy. If you stand at the source of a great river like the Thames you see nothing there but a tiny rivulet, the fact being that we do but by courtesy speak of that little brook as the source of the river. It is only a very partial source; a great river derives its volume of water from a thousand streams, and is sustained by the whole of the watershed along which it flows. The imaginary fountain-head of a river is therefore but a small affair, but suppose the Thames had never borrowed from a single stream in all its course, but welled up at once a full-grown river from some one fountain-head, what a sight it would be! Now the mercy of God to us in Christ Jesus owes nothing to any other stream, it leaps in all its fulness from the infinite depths of the love of God to us, and if in contemplation you can travel to that great deep, profound and unfathomable, and see welling up all the floods of covenant grace, which afterwards flow on for ever to all the chosen seed, you have before you that which angels wonder at. If it would be marvellous to see one river leap up from the earth full-grown, what would it be to gaze upon a vast spring from which all the rivers of the earth should at once come bubbling up, a thousand of them born at a birth? What a vision would it be! Who can conceive it! And yet the love of God is that fountain from which all the rivers of mercy which have ever gladdened our race—all the rivers of grace in time and of glory hereafter—take their rise. My soul, stand thou at that sacred fountain-head, and adore and magnify for ever and ever "God, even our Father, who hath loved us."

Now please to notice the words of the text, for they are full of instruction: when speaking of this love, the apostle joins our Lord Jesus Christ himself with "God, even our Father." He honoured the deity of Jesus by speaking of him side by side, and on terms of equality, with God the Father. But there is more here than this, for the words remind us that our Lord Jesus Christ and God, even our Father, act in holy concert in the matters which concern our welfare. Jesus Christ is the gift of the Father's love to us, but Jesus himself loved his own, and laid down his life for his sheep. It is true that the Son loves us, but the Father himself loveth us too. The love of God does not come to us from one person of the blessed Trinity alone,

174

but from all. We ought to make no distinctions by way of preference in the love of either Father, Son, or Holy Ghost. One love dwells in the breast of the one undivided Three, we must adore and bless our Lord Jesus Christ and God, even our Father, with equal gratitude.

Still notice that Jesus Christ is here put first, and if the reason be requested, we find it in his meditorial office. He is first to us in our experience. We began our dealings with heaven, not by going to the Father, but to his Son, Jesus Christ. Our Lord has truly said, "No man cometh unto the Father but by me." All attempts to get to commune with the Father, except through the Son, must be futile. Election by the Father is not first to us, though it stands forth in order of time; redemption by the Son is our starting point. Not at the throne of sovereignty, but at the cross of dying love, our spiritual life must date its birth. Look to Jesus first, even our Lord Jesus Christ; and then follow after the Father. I am sure every converted soul here knows that this is the truth, and I would exhort everyone who is seeking salvation, to take care to observe God's order, and remember that the love of the Father will never be perceived by us, nor felt in our hearts, till first of all we go to Jesus Christ, who is the one mediator between God and man.

Note the words of the text again: The love of God to us gives to us the Lord Jesus to be our own Saviour, friend, husband, and Lord. By grace we obtain possession of Jesus Christ—Christ is ours. Observe the word, "Our Lord Jesus Christ." The apostle might have written, "The Lord Jesus Christ;" but when he was testifying of the great love of God, the article would not have sufficed—he must use a word of possession. Faith looks to Jesus, and finds salvation in that look; then she grows into assurance, and having used her eyes to look with, she next employs her hands to grasp with. She takes hold of Jesus, and says: "He is all my salvation, he is all my desire, he is my Christ;" and henceforth assurance speaks not of the Lord Jesus Christ, but of our Lord Jesus Christ. I want you to drink into the love of God this morning from the silver pipe of this thought,—Jesus Christ the Son of the eternal God, who is also a man like yourself, is yours, altogether yours. If you be believers in him he is from head to foot entirely yours; in all his offices, in all his attributes, in all that he is, in all that he has done, in all that he is doing, in all that he shall do, he is your Saviour. Though you cannot take him up in your arms as Simeon did, yet can your faith embrace him with the like ecstasy, and feel that you have seen God's salvation. Behold what manner of love is revealed in this, that God should give his only Son to us. God commendeth his love to us by this unspeakable gift. Here love has reached its climax. Blessed be the love of God this morning, and for evermore.

Observe that this love displays itself in another shape, for the text goes on to say, "And God, even our Father." He might have said, "God, even the Father." I have no doubt the text does refer to the Father as one person of the blessed Trinity, but it runs thus: "even our Father." A father! There is music in that word, but not to a fatherless child—to him it is full of sorrowful memories. Those who have never lost a father can scarcely know how precious a relation a father is. A father, who is a father indeed, is very dear! Do we not remember how we climbed his knee? Do we not recollect the kisses we imprinted on his cheeks? Do we not recall to-day with gratitude the chidings of his wisdom and the gentle encouragements of his affection? We owe, ah! who shall tell how much we owe to our fathers according to the flesh, and when they are taken from us we lament their loss, and feel that a great gap is made in our family circle. Listen, then, to these words, "Our Father, who is in heaven." Consider the grace contained in the Lord's deigning to take us into the relationship of children, and giving us with the relationship the nature and the spirit of children, so that we say, "Abba, Father." Did you ever lie in bed with your limbs vexed with sore pains, and cry, "Father, pity thy child?" Did you ever look into the face of death, and as you thought you were about to depart, cry, "My Father, help me; uphold me with thy gracious hand, and bear me through the stream of death?" It is at such times that we realise the glory of the Fatherhood of God, and in our feebleness learn to cling to the divine strength, and catch at the divine love. It is most precious to think that God is our own Father! There, now, I cannot talk about it. Upon some themes it would be hard to be silent, but here it is hard to speak. I can but exclaim, "Behold, what manner of love the Father hath bestowed upon us that we should be called the children of God;" and, having said that, what more remains?

Before I turn from this gracious and fruitful topic of the love of God, I beg you to notice that it is no new thing, no affair of yesterday. "Our Lord Jesus Christ himself and God, even our Father, hath loved us;" he does not tell us when this began, and he could not have done so had he tried. He hath loved us; loved us when first we came to him repenting; loved us when we were spending our living with harlots; loved us when we were at the swine trough; loved us when from head to foot we were one mass of defilement. O God, didst thou love me when I played the rebel—love me when I could blaspheme thy name? What manner of love is this? Ay, and he loved us ere we had a being; loved us and redeemed us long before we existed; loved us ere this world had sprung out of nothingness; loved us ere the day-star first proclaimed the morning; loved us ere any of the angels had begun to cover their faces with their wings in reverent adoration. From everlasting, the Lord loved his people. Now, again I say, drink into this truth, feed on it; expect us not to expatiate thereon, but contemplate the fact—"Jesus Christ, and God, even our Father, hath loved us."

II. Now we shall turn to the second point, which is THE MANIFESTATIONS OF THIS LOVE. They divide under two heads—"everlasting consolation" and "good hope through grace."

First, God's love has given us everlasting consolation. The Lord found us wretched; when the arrows of conviction were sticking in our hearts we were bleeding to death, and what we wanted, first of all, was to have these wounds staunched; therefore the Lord came to us with consolations. Remember ye not the time when the blood of Jesus Christ flowed warm over your wounds and made them cease to bleed? Have you forgotten the hour when you heard the voice of the Lord saying in the word, "Whosoever believeth in him is not condemned," and you were enabled to see Jesus Christ as your substitute suffering in your room and stead, and you knew that your sins were forgiven for his name's sake? You have not forgotten that? Well, that was one of the everlasting consolations which he gave you in the time of your distress. Since that day you have had your sorrows, perhaps you have been seldom long without them; but consolation has always followed on the heels of tribulation, and your main consolation has continued to be where it was at the first; you still find the sweetest joy of earth to be looking unto Jesus. When sin rebels you put it down by the self-same grace which overthrew it at the first. Conscience starts and accuses you, and you answer its accusations with that sweet word, "Jesus died for our transgressions, and rose again for our justification." The greatest delight of all is, that this consolation is an everlasting one—other sources of comfort dry up; friends have called to visit you in times of distress, and have suggested pleasant thoughts that have whiled away a mournful hour; but your griefs have returned again, and the passing comfort has been of no further service to you. When a man sees that Jesus Christ took all his sins, and was punished for them, so that the man himself never can be punished again—when he understands that wondrous mystery of substitution, then he gets a consolation which serves him at all times, and in all weathers. Whatever may occur to him he flies to this refuge; and even though he may have fallen into great sin, he knows that the atonement was not made for sham sin, but for real sin; and he resorts again to that same fountain filled with blood, wherein he was once washed, resting fully assured that it will be equal to the washing of him as long as he shall be capable of sin. "Everlasting consolation!" There are some here present who have tried this consolation for forty or fifty years; dear brethren and sisters, I am sure you do not find it is any the weaker, but on the contrary you understand more of its strength. You are more happy to-day in falling back upon the love of God than you were, and at this moment you feel that in the absence of all other comforts it would suffice you to know that everlasting consolation which is given you in Christ Jesus.

Let us run over for a moment some of our consolations. The first one is, as I have already said, that God hath forgiven us all our transgressions, because Jesus died in our stead. The next consolation is that God loves us, and can never change in his love:—

> "Whom once he loves he never leaves,
>
> But loves them to the end."

Then we have the grand consolation that the promises of God do not depend upon our faithfulness for their fulfilment but are all stablished and made yea and amen in Christ Jesus. We have this consolation—that our salvation does not depend upon ourselves: as we fell and were lost by the first Adam's unrighteousness, so we have risen and are saved through the second Adam's righteousness, beyond all risk and fear of perishing. We stand upon a firm foundation, not on the shifting sand of creature obedience and faithfulness, but upon the eternal rock of a work which Christ has completed, and over which he sang that joyous pæan,—"It is finished," ere he entered into his rest.

We have also this consolation, that all things work together for good for us who love God and are the called according to his purpose; and again this other consolation, that as long as Christ exists we are as safe, for he has said, "Because I live, ye shall live also." We have this consolation also, that even though we shall sleep in the dust for awhile, yet he hath said it, "I will that they also whom thou hast given me be with me where I am that they may behold my glory." In fact, to tell you all the consolations which God has given us would need many an hour, and fully to enjoy them will occupy your entire lives, for everlasting consolation is not to be spread out before you and done with in the short space of a discourse. Thus much upon one of the first manifestations of divine love.

The next is, he has given us "good hope." Consolation for the present, hope for the future. "Good hope," the hope when days and years are past we all shall meet in heaven; the hope that whatever the future may be, it is full of bliss for us; the hope of immortality for our souls, and of resurrection for our bodies, for when Christ shall come, we also that sleep in Jesus shall come with him. The hope of reigning with Jesus Christ on earth in the days of his triumph, and reigning with him for ever and ever in endless felicity. This is our hope, a good hope, for it is based and founded on a good foundation. A fanatic's hope will pass away with the vapours which produced it, but the hope of the true believer is good because it is founded in truth and in grace. "A good hope in grace," is the Greek. If I believed in my own merit, and based my hopes thereon, I should be only self-deceived and blinded, for what merit have I? But if my hope be fixed alone in grace, and that be the sphere in which my consolation and hope are found, then, since God is assuredly gracious, since he has made a covenant of grace with all believers, since he has ratified the covenant by the gift of his own Son, and since he has sworn by his holiness that he will not lie unto David, a hope founded on his grace is a good hope. Since God will be as good as his word, his hope in grace is good. Here stands the fact: it is written, "he that believeth in the Lord Jesus hath everlasting life." God has covenanted with that man that he shall be saved eternally, and since God cannot lie, the believing man must and shall be saved. Why is it then that some believer's hopes flicker? Because they get away from a hope in grace, and look towards themselves and their own merits. "Oh," they say, "I have not prayed as I did, I do not feel as I did, therefore, my hope declines." Friend, was your hope founded on your prayers? was your hope grounded in part upon your feelings? If so, it may well quiver and tremble; one of these days it will go down altogether, for the foundation is not able to bear its weight. But if my hope is fixed on this, that God hath promised, and cannot change his promise, I have a good bottom to build on. He will not alter the thing that has gone forth out of his lips: he hath said, "he that believeth and is baptised shall be saved," and he cannot change his own word; therefore every believer has the promise of eternal life. "But," saith one, "it surprises me to hear you talk so." Does it? It much more surprises me that I may so speak. It is marvellous to the last degree that God, even our Father, and the Lord Jesus Christ should have given us such a hope as this. I never feel at all astonished at some people's hope when I find that it is this—the hope that if they behave themselves they will get to heaven; the hope that if they are faithful, God will be faithful. Why! Any simpleton might have imagined such a hope as that; but a divine revelation was needed to set before us the great hope of the gospel, and it needs grace-given faith to believe that God will not change nor lie, and, therefore, must save all those who have believed in his Son Jesus Christ. He cannot suffer one of the sheep of Christ to perish, or his promise will be of none effect. "If I believed that," saith one, "it would cause me to lead a careless life." Perhaps it would, but it does not lead true believers to do so; on the contrary, we feel that if God loves us so, and deals so generously with us, and takes us right away from the whips of Sinai and the covenant of the law, and places us entirely under grace, we love him as we never loved before, and because of that love sin is hateful to us, and we shun it as a deadly thing! The law which you think would drive men to holiness has never done it, while the grace which you imagine would lead us to licentiousness binds us with solemn bonds of consecration to serve our God ten times more than before! Suppose some one were to tell my children that the continuance of my love to them will depend entirely upon their good behaviour. My children would repel the suggestion with indignation. They would answer, "we know better; you speak falsely; our father will always love us." Even so the Lord's children know that their Father's love is immutable. For our transgressions, our heavenly Father will visit us with the rod, but never with the sword. He will be angry with us, and chide us, but he will love us just as much when he is angry as he did before; and as long as ever we are his sons—and that we always must be, for sonship is not a relationship which will ever change—so long will he love us. Do you think that children become disobedient because their relationship is unchangeable? I never heard of such a thing. They have many reasons for being disobedient within their own little wayward hearts, but no child disobeys his father because he always must be his father's child, or because his father loves him. I have heard of one child who said to another, "Come with me, John, and rob such an orchard; your father is so kind he will not beat you if you are found out." The little lad drew himself up, and said, "Do you think because my father is kind to me that, therefore, I will go and vex him?" This is the holy reasoning of love; it draws no license from grace, but rather feels the strong constraints of gratitude leading it to holiness. It may be that in unregenerate hearts the love of God, if it could come there, would be turned into an excuse for sin; but it is not so to us, my brethren. Since the grace of God has made us new creatures in Christ Jesus, the love of God constraineth us not to sin but to walk in holiness all our days. Blessed be his name, then; we are not ashamed to rejoice that God, even our Father, hath loved us, and given us everlasting consolation and good hope in grace.

III. The last thing is THE PRAYER flowing out of all this. The apostle prays, and we pray this morning, that God would comfort your hearts. This is not spoken of everybody, but of such as believe in the Lord Jesus. It is of the utmost importance that your hearts should be comforted. Cheerfulness, habitual calm, peace of mind, content of spirit,—these ought to be the very atmosphere you breathe; and Paul thinks it so important that he prays that God himself, and Christ himself, may comfort your hearts. I know you have many troubles—how very few are altogether without them! Some of you are very poor, others suffer heavy losses in business, and exercises of soul, with much trial in the world and in the church. May the good Lord comfort your hearts, speaking not to your ears only, but to your innermost nature. "Let not your heart be troubled, neither let it be afraid." Why, surely, if you believe that God loves you, it ought to make your heart glad; and if he gives you everlasting consolation you cannot be otherwise than happy. I remember well when I was under a sense of sin looking at a dog and wishing I were such as he, that I might die without fear of judgment hereafter, for it seemed so awful a thing to live on for ever as a sinner; but now, on the other hand, I have sometimes looked at the happiest animals, and I have said to myself, "Ah, but yonder poor creature does not know the love of God, and how thankful I am to God that he has given me the capacity to know himself Why, if I could hear of an angel in heaven who did not know the love of God I should pity him. There are kings and mighty emperors who know not the Lord's love, and what poor, pitiable creatures they are. But as for you who rejoice in divine love, I would have you go into the darkest alley if you are forced to live there, and undergo the most wearisome toil if that be your lot—ay, and go home to a persecuting husband, or a churlish father, and yet hear melodious music ringing in your hearts, for "God, even our Father, which hath loved us, hath given us everlasting consolation and good hope through grace." This is enough to make the wilderness rejoice and blossom as the rose.

The next part of the prayer is that the "Lord would stablish us in every good word and work." I see that the most approved editions of the original have it, "in every good work and word," putting the best first; and the thought is this, that God would make his people so happy that they would never have an inclination to leave off any good work or word. Depression of spirit often leads to slackness of hand. No doubt many, through sad hearts, have ceased to labour for Christ. A want of gladness has restrained their activity. Now, the apostle would not have any one of us cease from serving God in good works or in good words through a want of consolation. Does God love you? Do you know it? How then can you cease from any good work? Did enemies abuse you for speaking the truth? Did you say it because you felt you loved God? Say it again, man! Say it again! Did you work in your class without success? Did you do it because God loved you and you wanted to shew that you loved him? Go on, brother! go on, sister! success or no success! God loves you and he has given you everlasting consolation, therefore be stablished in your good work. Have you been accustomed to sing his praises, and has the devil said, "Leave off! leave off!" Have you been accustomed to rebuke sin, and to tell others about the Saviour in your own poor way, and are you getting low in spirit? Do you doubt your own interest in Christ? Have you lost the comfort you once enjoyed? O, dear brother, come back to the old original source of happiness—"Jesus Christ himself, and God, even our Father, which hath loved us, and given us everlasting consolation and good hope through grace." After refreshing yourself with this blessed truth, you will return with renewed energy to good words and works, and continue in them steadfast, unmoveable, till life's allotted service shall come to a close.

Now and then we become greatly disheartened about the condition of the church. I know I do. I see everywhere Popery spreading, or else rationalism—these rival evils are devouring our country. There is far too little prayerfulness, and too little gospel preaching; and at times, one is apt to cry out, like Elijah, that no one is left who is faithful to Jehovah—all knees are bowed to Baal! We must not give way to this feeling, dear friends, for "God, even the Father, hath loved us." When the disciples were too much elated with their success, and came back to Jesus, and said, "Lord, even the devils are subject unto us," Jesus said, "Notwithstanding, in this rejoice not, but rather rejoice because your names are written in heaven." And to-day, when we are depressed with great anxieties, and come back to our Master, and say, "Lord, the devil is getting the upper hand over us;" he repeats to us the self-same admonition, "Nevertheless do not be depressed about this, but rather rejoice because your names are written in heaven, and your Father hath given you everlasting consolation, and good hope through grace."

Stablish your hearts, then, beloved brethren. Be ye "stedfast, unmoveable, always abounding in the work of the Lord." Things are not what they seem. Dark nights are but the prelude to bright days. The rain shall be followed by the clear shining. When truth retreats, she only retires to leap to a greater victory. Though each wave as it comes up upon the shore may die, and you may think that there is no progress, yet the tide is coming in, even Jehovah's tide of everlasting truth which shall cover all the earth. Be not discouraged! Go to your God. Get away, every man, from your circumstances and from your selves, and get to your

Saviour and your Shepherd; and there, like sheep in the pasture, lie down to feed; and then, like sheep obedient to the shepherd, rise up and follow him withersoever he goeth. God bless you in this.

Perhaps while I have been preaching, some unconverted person here has been saying—"There is nothing for me." Do you remember, dear friend, what the Syro-Phœnician woman said? She was called a dog by the Saviour, and that is what you think your are, but she said, "The dogs eat the crumbs that fall from the Master's table." Now, if I called myself a dog, would there be anything in this subject that I might dare to lay hold upon, because, like a crumb, it fell from the table? Yes. It seems to me there is. Evidently God deals with his own people in a way of grace, for it is said, he has "given" us—it is altogether of his free love, and it added—"through grace," or absolute favour. The consolations of the Lord are the gifts of mercy and love; well, then, if he is gracious to one, why should not he be gracious to another? And if those who sit at his table were once unclean, and filthy, and depraved, and yet the sovereign grace of God called them and brought them into the banquet of love, why should it not light on me also? If it is not of him that willeth nor of him that runneth, but of God that showeth mercy, why should he not show mercy to me, whoever I may be? Why not to me?

But is there a door through which I can come to the gracious Lord? Yes, there is, and it is the other crumb in the text, for it begins with "our Lord Jesus Christ." My soul, that is where thou must begin this morning. There is the Lord Jesus Christ. I see him hanging on the cross bleeding for the sins of others, with hands stretched wide that he may receive sinners to his heart, and that heart has a channel made down to it by the spear, that prayers and tears may find an easy way into his sympathies. Come, my soul, come now, and tell thy case to Jesus. Fellow-sinner, come and confess thy sin to Jesus, and then throw thyself at his feet with this upon thy heart and lips—"If I must perish, I will perish clinging to the cross, declaring to all men that my hope is stayed on him whom God has set forth to be the propitiation for the sins of man." You will never perish there, sinner. Go there at once, and be safe. God help you for Christ's sake. Amen.

APPENDIX:
A COMPLETE LIST OF
THE APOSTLE PAUL'S PRAYERS

First, I thank my God through Jesus Christ for all of you, because your faith is being reported all over the world. God, whom I serve with my whole heart in preaching the gospel of his Son, is my witness how constantly I remember you in my prayers at all times; and I pray that now at last by God's will the way may be opened for me to come to you. [Romans 1:8–10]

Brothers, my heart's desire and prayer to God for the Israelites is that they may be saved. [Romans 10:1]

Be joyful in hope, patient in affliction, faithful in prayer. [Romans 12:12]

May the God who gives endurance and encouragement give you a spirit of unity among yourselves as you follow Christ Jesus, so that with one heart and mouth you may

glorify the God and Father of our Lord Jesus Christ.
[Romans 15:5–6]

May the God of hope fill you with all joy and peace as you trust in him, so that you may overflow with hope by the power of the Holy Spirit. [Romans 15:13]

I urge you, brothers, by our Lord Jesus Christ and by the love of the Spirit, to join me in my struggle by praying to God for me. Pray that I may be rescued from the unbelievers in Judea and that my service in Jerusalem may be acceptable to the saints there, so that by God's will I may come to you with joy and together with you be refreshed. The God of peace be with you all. Amen. [Romans 15:30–33]

I always thank God for you because of his grace given you in Christ Jesus. For in him you have been enriched in every way— in all your speaking and in all your knowledge— because our testimony about Christ was confirmed in you. Therefore you do not lack any spiritual gift as you eagerly wait for our Lord Jesus Christ to be revealed. He will keep you strong to the end, so that you will be blameless on the day of our Lord Jesus Christ. God, who has called you into fellowship with his Son Jesus Christ our Lord, is faithful. [1 Corinthians 1:4–9]

The grace of the Lord Jesus be with you. [1 Corinthians 16:23]

Praise be to the God and Father of our Lord Jesus Christ, the Father of compassion and the God of all comfort, who comforts us in all our troubles, so that we can comfort those in any trouble with the comfort we ourselves have received from God. For just as the sufferings of Christ flow over into our lives, so also through Christ our comfort overflows. If we are distressed, it is for your comfort and salvation; if we are comforted, it is for your comfort, which produces in you patient endurance of the same sufferings we suffer. And our hope for you is firm, because we know that just as you share in our sufferings, so also you share in our comfort. [2 Corinthians 1:3–7]

But thanks be to God, who always leads us in triumphal procession in Christ and through us spreads everywhere the fragrance of the knowledge of him. For we are to God the aroma of Christ among those who are being saved and those who are perishing. To the one we are the smell of death; to the other, the fragrance of life. And who is equal to such a task? [2 Corinthians 2:14–16]

This service that you perform is not only supplying the needs of God's people but is also overflowing in many expressions of thanks to God. Because of the service by which you have proved yourselves, men will praise God for the obedience that accompanies your confession of the gospel of Christ, and for your generosity in sharing with them and with everyone else. And in their prayers for you their hearts will go out to you, because of the surpassing grace God has give you. Thanks be to God for his indescribable gift! [2 Corinthians 9:12–15]

To keep me from becoming conceited because of these surpassingly great revelations, there was given me a thorn in my flesh, a messenger of Satan, to torment me. Three times I pleaded with the Lord to take it away from me. But he said to me, "My grace is sufficient for you, for my power is made perfect in weakness." [2 Corinthians 12:7–9a]

Now we pray to God that you will not do anything wrong. Not that people will see that we have stood the test but that you will do what is right even though we may seem to have failed. For we cannot do anything against the truth, but only for the truth. We are glad whenever we are weak but you are strong; and our prayer is for your perfection. [2 Corinthians 13:7–9]

The grace of our Lord Jesus Christ be with your spirit, brothers. [Galatians 6:18]

Praise be to the God and Father of our Lord Jesus Christ, who has blessed us in the heavenly realms with every spiritual blessing in Christ. For he chose us in him before the creation of the world to be holy and blameless in his sight. In love he predestined us to be adopted as his sons through Jesus Christ, in accordance with his pleasure and will—to the praise of his glorious grace, which he has freely given us in the One he loves. In him we have redemption through his blood, the forgiveness of sins, in accordance with the riches of God's grace that he lavished on us with all wisdom and understanding. . . . [Ephesians 1:3ff]

For this reason, ever since I heard about your faith in the Lord Jesus and your love for all the saints, I have not stopped giving thanks for you, remembering you in my prayers. I keep asking that the God of our Lord Jesus Christ, the glorious Father, may give you the Spirit of wisdom and revelation, so that you may know him better. I pray also that the eyes of your heart may be enlightened in order that you may know the hope to which he has called you, the riches of his glorious inheritance in the saints, and his incomparably great power for us who believe. That power is like the working of his mighty strength, which he exerted in Christ when he raised him from the dead and seated him at his right hand in the heavenly realms, far above all rule and authority, power and dominion, and every title that can be given, not only in the present age but also in the one to come. And God placed all things under his feet and appointed him to be head over everything for the church, which is his body, the fullness of him who fills everything in every way. [Ephesians 1:15–23]

For this reason, I kneel before the Father, from whom his whole family in heaven and on earth derives its name. I pray that out of his glorious riches he may strengthen you with power through his Spirit in your inner being, so that Christ may dwell in your hearts through faith. And I pray that you, being rooted and established in love, may have power, together with all the saints, to grasp how wide and long and high and deep is the love of Christ, and to know this love that surpasses knowledge—that you may be filled to the measure of all the fullness of God. Now to him who is able to do immeasurably more than all we ask or imagine, according to his power that is at work within us, to him be glory in the church and in Christ Jesus throughout all generations, for ever and ever! Amen. [Ephesians 3:14–21]

Pray also for me, that whenever I open my mouth, words may be given me so that I will fearlessly make known the mystery of the gospel, for which I am an ambassador in chains. Pray that I may declare it fearlessly, as I should. [Ephesians 6:19–20]

I thank my God every time I remember you. In all my prayers for all of you, I always pray with joy because of your partnership in the gospel from the first day until now, being confident of this, that he who began a good work in you will carry it on to completion until the day of Christ Jesus. [Philippians 1:3–6]

And this is my prayer: that your love may abound more and more in knowledge and depth of insight, so that you may be able to discern what is best and may be pure and blameless until the day of Christ, filled with the fruit of righteousness that comes through Jesus Christ—to the glory and praise of God. [Philippians 1:9–11]

Do not be anxious about anything, but in everything, by prayer and petition, with thanksgiving, present your requests to God. And the peace of God, which transcends all understanding, will guard your hearts and your minds in Christ Jesus. [Phil. 4:6–7]

The grace of the Lord Jesus Christ be with your spirit. Amen. [Philippians 4:23]

We always thank God the Father of our Lord Jesus Christ, when we pray for you, because we have heard of your faith in Christ Jesus and of the love you have for all the saints—the faith and love that spring from the hope that is stored up for you in heaven and that you have already heard about in the word of truth, the gospel that has come to you. All over the world this gospel is bearing fruit and growing, just as it has been doing among you since the day you heard it and understood God's grace in all its truth. You learned it from Epaphras, our dear fellow servant, who is a faithful minister of Christ on our behalf, and who also told us of your love in the Spirit. For this reason, since the day we heard about you, we have not stopped praying for you and asking God to fill you with the knowledge of his will through all spiritual wisdom and understanding. And we pray this in order that you may live a life worthy of the Lord and may please him in every way: bearing fruit in every good work, growing in the knowledge of God, being strengthened with all power according to his glorious might so that you may have great endurance and patience, and joyfully giving thanks to the Father, who has qualified you to share in the inheritance of the saints in the kingdom of light. For he has rescued us from the dominion of darkness and brought us into the kingdom of the Son he loves, in whom we have redemption, the forgiveness of sins. [Colossians 1:3–14]

Devote yourselves to prayer, being watchful and thankful. And pray for us, too, that God may open a door for our message, so that we may proclaim the mystery of Christ, for which I am in chains. Pray that I may proclaim it clearly, as I should. [Colossians 4:2–4]

We always thank God for all of you, mentioning you in our prayers. We continually remember before our God and Father your work produced by faith, your labor prompted by love, and your endurance inspired by hope in our Lord Jesus Christ. [1 Thessalonians 1:2–3]

And we also thank God continually because, when you received the word of God, which you heard from us, you accepted it not as the word of men, but as it actually is, the word of God, which is at work in you who believe. For you, brothers, became imitators of God's churches in Judea, which are in Christ Jesus: You suffered from your own countrymen the same things those churches suffered from the Jews, who killed the Lord Jesus and the prophets and also drove us out. They displease God and are hostile to all men in their effort to keep us from speaking to the Gentiles so that they may be saved. In this way they always heap up their sins to the limit. The wrath of God has come upon them at last. [1 Thessalonians 2:13–16]

How can we thank God enough for you in return for all the joy we have in the presence of our God because of you? Night and day we pray most earnestly that we may see you again and supply what is lacking in your faith. Now may our God and Father himself and our Lord Jesus clear the way for us to come to you. May the Lord make your love increase and overflow for each other and for everyone else, just as ours does for you. May he strengthen your hearts so that you will be blameless and holy in the presence of our God and Father when our Lord Jesus comes with all his holy ones. [1 Thessalonians 3:9–13]

May God himself, the God of peace, sanctify you through and through. May your whole spirit, soul and body be kept blameless at the coming of our Lord Jesus Christ. The one who calls you is faithful and he will do it. [1 Thessalonians 5:23–24]

The grace of our Lord Jesus Christ be with you. [1 Thessalonians 5:28]

We ought always to thank God for you, brothers, and rightly so, because your faith is growing more and more, and the love every one of you has for each other is increasing. Therefore, among God's churches we boast about your perseverance and faith in all the persecutions and trials you are enduring. . . . [2 Thessalonians 1:3ff]

With this in mind, we constantly pray for you, that our God may count you worthy of his calling, and that by his power he may fulfill every good purpose of yours and every act prompted by your faith. We pray this so that the name of our Lord Jesus may be glorified in you, and you in him, according to the grace of our God and the Lord Jesus Christ. [2 Thessalonians 1:11–12]

May our Lord Jesus Christ himself and God our Father, who loved us and by his grace gave us eternal encouragement and good hope, encourage your hearts and strengthen you in every good deed and word. [2 Thessalonians 2:16–17]

And pray that we may be delivered from wicked and evil men, for not everyone has faith. But the Lord is faithful, and he will strengthen and protect you from the evil one. We have confidence in the Lord that you are doing and will continue to do the things we command. May the Lord direct your hearts into God's love and Christ's perseverance. [2 Thessalonians 3:2–5]

Now may the Lord of peace himself give you peace at all times and in every way. The Lord be with all of you. [2 Thessalonians 3:16]

I thank Christ Jesus our Lord, who has given me strength, that he considered me faithful, appointing me to his service. [1 Timothy 1:12]

I urge, then, first of all, that requests, prayers, intercession and thanksgiving be made for everyone—for kings and all those in authority, that we may live peaceful and quiet lives in all godliness and holiness. This is good, and pleases God our Savior, who wants all men to be saved and to come to a knowledge of the truth. For there is one God and one mediator between God and men, the man Christ Jesus, who gave himself as a ransom for all men—the testimony given in its proper time. . . . [1 Timothy 2:1ff]

I thank God, whom I serve, as my forefathers did, with a clear conscience, as night and day I constantly remember you in my prayers. Recalling your tears, I long to see you, so that I may be filled with joy. I have been reminded of your sincere faith, which first lived in your grandmother Lois and in your mother Eunice and, I am persuaded, now lives in you also. For this reason I remind you to fan into flame the gift of God which is in you through the laying on of my hands. For God did not give us a spirit of timidity, but a spirit of power, of love and of self-discipline. [2 Timothy 1:3–7]

May the Lord show mercy to the household of Onesiphorus, because he often refreshed me and was not ashamed of my chains. On the contrary, when he was in

Rome, he searched hard for me until he found me. May the Lord grant that he will find mercy from the Lord on that day! You know very well in how many ways he helped me in Ephesus. [2 Timothy 1:16–18]

The Lord be with your spirit. Grace be with you. [2 Timothy 4:22]

Grace be with you all. [Titus 3:15b]

I always thank my God as I remember you in my prayers, because I hear about your faith in the Lord Jesus and your love for all the saints. I pray that you may be active in sharing your faith, so that you will have a full understanding of every good thing we have in Christ. Your love has given me great joy and encouragement, because you, brother, have refreshed the hearts of the saints. [Philemon 4–7]

The grace of the Lord Jesus Christ be with your spirit. [Philemon 25]

—

ABOUT THE AUTHOR

Charles Haddon Spurgeon, known as "The Prince of Preachers", was a famous Reformed Baptist preacher born in Essex, England in 1834. A full-time preacher by the age of 17, Spurgeon preached an estimated 3,600 sermons by the time of his death in 1892. Spurgeon frequently preached to audiences larger than 10,000, while his printed sermons reached tens of thousands more each week.

Spurgeon authored almost 50 volumes including the classic works *All of Grace, Morning & Evening, The Power of Prayer in a Believer's Life, Lectures to My Students,* and *The Treasury of David: A Commentary on the Psalms.* More than a century after his death, Spurgeon's devotional writings continue to touch hearts around the world. Once when asked the secret of his success, Spurgeon replied, "My people pray for me."

MINISTRIES WE LOVE

Cross-Points Books loves organizations committed to building Christ's church by proclaiming the gospel, resourcing leaders, and training workers for the harvest. Here are some of our favorite ministries:

9Marks — Building Healthy Churches (www.9marks.org)

Desiring God — Helping people understand and embrace the truth that God is most glorified in us when we are most satisfied in him. (www.desiringgod.org)

Matthias Media — An evangelical publisher of gospel-centered resources. (www.matthiasmedia.com)

Leadership Resources — A global ministry training pastors in 30+ countries to preach expository sermons, train other expositors, and foster movements of God's Word. (www.leadershipresources.org)

The Gospel Coalition — Encouraging and educating Christian leaders by advocating gospel-centered principles and practices that glorify the Savior and do good to those for whom he shed his life's blood. (www.thegospelcoalition.org)

The Spurgeon Center — Making visible the life, legacy, and library of Charles Haddon Spurgeon. (center.spurgeon.org)

Unlocking the Bible — Delivering the gospel through modern media. The teaching ministry of Colin S. Smith. (www.unlockingthebible.org)

CONNECT WITH CROSS-POINTS

For news on upcoming releases and deals on resources
promoting sound doctrine and godly devotion,
visit Cross-Points.org or follow us on social media.

54327348R00126